Supernatural Is Natural

A Book
by
Rosemarie Campione

As Told to

Legh Townsend

Supernatural Is Natural

by Rosemarie Campione as told to
Legh Townsend

iUniverse, Inc.
New York Lincoln Shanghai

Supernatural Is Natural

iUniverse books may be ordered through booksellers or by contacting:

iUniverse
2021 Pine Lake Road, Suite 100
Lincoln, NE 68512
www.iuniverse.com
1-800-Authors (1-800-288-4677)

ISBN: 978-0-595-46533-0 (pbk)
ISBN: 978-0-595-70514-6 (cloth)
ISBN: 978-0-595-90830-1 (ebk)

Printed in the United States of America

Contents

Part III THE FUNCTIONING ENTITY

Foreword

by Rosemarie Campione, Ph.D.

Although most of this work is my story, it is a combination of my thoughts and those of my very dear friend, Legh Townsend. She has lovingly listened to my talks and assembled my writings, adding the wisdom of her many years in metaphysics, and put it all down in the pages within this volume.

A friendship bordering on forty years has given us many opportunities for in-depth discussion on various philosophies and the so-called supernatural. Our views and beliefs follow similar journeys to enlightenment. We have reached identical solutions on many issues having to do with the subjects covered here.

While this book was still in the composition stage I had a stroke that incapacitated me for over a year. I had just about gotten my self back when I was hit with another, more debilitating one, that affected my memory in drastic ways. Two years later when my friend told me we were writing a book, my comment was, "we are?" I did not remember.

This has been over ten years in progress with many setbacks, but here it is, Dear Reader, with my best wishes.

Introduction

by Legh Townsend, Ph.D.

Curiosity in what the future may bring has always had a powerful influence in our lives. Should I marry him/her? Take this job? Buy this house? Within each of us lies the potential of tapping into the frontier of the mind to see the clear possibilities for future happenings.

This is a story of one psychic who developed her abilities into a counseling career of a lifetime with a vast clientele. She has taught psychic classes to hundreds of students interested in exploring and utilizing their paranormal occurrences. Practice and research into every form of psychodynamics has brought about a belief that every aspect may be used in order to enhance quality and enjoyment of life.

Rosemarie and I worked together on many of her speaking engagements. Having similar interests in the paranormal I urged her to write her story, including the many psychic experiences she has had over the years. After trying to find time to write, giving up and hiring a ghostwriter who gave up after discovering there wasn't an interest there, I offered my writing skills and thoughts.

When we discussed writing this book, we agreed that the biggest deterrent in giving attention to psychic breakthroughs was fear. Fear of the unknown raises its head when there is talk or happenings that cannot be explained or defined. These gifts that are inherent in all of us are natural, just as dreaming, creating or merely thinking.

By relating her firsthand knowledge of actual events and explorations and her reactions at the time, we attempt to demonstrate to the reader that living psychically is possible and even beneficial to humans. There are many ways to receive these gifts. Some are specific to the person, such as precognitive feelings, visions or sound. Also, symbols play a large part in the interpretation of these messages, and are personal to the receptor. The various methods can be studied and applied to our daily lives.

Discovering your unique talent is a process of trial and error, research into other psychics' methods, and confirmation of what is suspected or learned in psychic exploration.

After reading this book it is hoped that the reader will have a greater understanding of what paranormal experiences are, how they are interpreted, and how they may be implemented.

"... There are no natural or supernatural phenomena,
only very large gaps in our knowledge of what is natural ...
We should strive to fill those gaps of ignorance."
Edgar D. Mitchell, Apollo 14 Astronaut

PART I

BELIEFS AND PHILOSOPHIES

1

Energy

Everything is energy—and only energy.

A journey into the naturalness of the supernatural must begin with information about energy. I believe that everything is energy, from the smallest cell to the universe itself. Everything we see, hear or touch is a product of energy.

Webster defines the word *energy* as a "vigorous exertion of power; also, the resources that produce that power." The dictionary goes on to say that energy is "the quantum state of electrons in atoms and molecules."

Energy never changes, but it has the power to change everything.

Always creating, always moving, it is the stuff from which we are shaped. One form of energy can be changed to produce an entirely different form. The energy of heat, for example, can be used to generate steam, another form of energy. Steam then can build up pressure, forcing movement of objects. This is all energy "in action!"

What if all this energy is God?

When I was growing up I was curious about everything. I wanted to know how I came to be on this earth, why the sun came up every morning, how the bees made honey, what made the water in the stream run one way and not the other, etc., etc. I'm surprised that my nickname did not become "Why!" Some things I just figured out for myself and then later either confirmed or disproved my theories.

Through a process of research and deep thought I came to a few conclusions for myself which worked for the individual me.

The energy that we use seems to be limitless and readily available, around, in and through all living things. The meaning of energy in the scientific world correlates with everyday meaning of life itself. We see energy in everything around us. It is not difficult to describe a person who is filled with energy, or a person who seems to lack energy. Energy is movement, it is growth, it is heat, it is light in motion. It is said that all of the energy in the Universe never lessens; we can use it and it is still there!

I believe that everything that IS exists through various vibrations of one Energy on different levels. In all that we perceive, taste, smell, feel, hear, there is always molecular activity going on, each particle vibrating at its unique rate. If we cut a hunk out of a tree and view a cross-section under a strong microscope, we will see movement of particles. This is energy! This is Life!

Life. Pure Energy. I choose to call the One Energy, God. It is present in every single thing in our Universe. There is nothing that is outside of this Energy, or God. So, everything that IS, is God. God is in It, through It, of It. This is not a startling innovation, of course, but it is important to remember when you are working with psychic levels.

We think a thought, consciously or unconsciously. The thought is energy and vibrates on a deep level. Always in motion and creating, it eventually manifests on our level of human perception as "reality." Sometimes it is solid; sometimes it appears as a happening or event; sometimes it materializes into a person or animal; sometimes it is merely a changing of atoms to affect a condition of health or sickness. Thought is continually manifesting into something we call "real" on this human level of existence.

Stephen Hawking in his book, "*A Brief History of Time,*" writes:

"… everything in the universe, including light and gravity, can be described in terms of particles."

The essence of what Rabbi Abraham Heschel talked about the nature of God and man was that scientifically we appear as separate beings, and to the microscopic eye the cells contained within are seen as split particles, the universal, analytical viewpoint as the known and the unknown. However, in the mystical thought everything is seen as one energy.

We, as physical human beings, resonate on a certain level of Energy that keeps our bodies together, and puts the millions and millions of particles into one receptacle. I believe that we incarnate as containments, or vehicles, for a deeper part of us that lives within us, the soul, if you will. This soul vibrates on another level, but it needs a physical vessel to experience this very brief period of time in its evolution.

We get into conflict with ourselves when we think that we are the personality; that I am Rosemarie, you are John, and we live in a house in a city and own a car, have jobs and a closet full of clothes. That is how we identify ourselves. That is what most humans believe we are. I believe that we are souls that develop personalities in this lifetime to carry out our journey, the journey being a process to accomplish our soul's purpose.

If we pay attention to our souls we will know peace of mind, inner contentment and we will experience our lives in awe and wonder. If we are convinced that our personalities are who we really are, we usually have a lot of struggle and discordance between the self and the soul, because it is as though we are going against the natural grain, the natural flow of our life's plan.

I am asked frequently where I "get" the information for my psychic readings. There is nothing mysterious about it. At this time of my life I can say this, after over forty years of search and research! There is no mystery!

When I close my eyes and begin to breathe deeply, I am altering levels of vibration. I consciously turn off the chattering left hemisphere of my brain, which vibrates at a particular level, to permit me to analyze and choose. I place my attention on the psychic ability, which is housed in the right hemisphere and controls dreams and creativity, and allow it to enhance and express itself. Then, I shed the beta consciousness where I use my five senses and concentrate. When I feel I am centered enough I tune into another level of Energy. It is just another level of Energy that is available to everyone who is willing to make the connection.

The steps that I have perfected for me include: I ask the body to relax with the eyes closed, softly looking upward, *knowing* how much I am loved and grateful to be an instrument. I internally speak the client's first name and wait. I then can see, hear or feel the client in his/her totality.

Throughout the years that I have used my psychic senses I have been in touch with discarnate, out-of-body, entities that have come through and assisted me on the path of awareness. They will be described in another part of this book, as well as how and when they came into my realization.

When I pick up your "past life," I really am not sure that it was your past life, or what it is. The information just flows to me, and goes from me, for the benefit of the person I am attempting to assist. Most of the time I do not retain any knowledge of what I say.

Early on, when I first began to use my gifts, I would sometimes ruin my children's sharing of the day's happenings by "knowing" before being told what the outcome had been.

I suffered along with the people I was counseling at first because I did not know how to stop or to mask the information from my own consciousness. I learned to stop information received in a session by asking my unconscious mind to "forget" what I received during that hour, unless it directly concerned me, or my soul's growth.

We use time here on earth as a measuring device, but how do we know that everything isn't happening on many different levels right here and right now? And how do we know that we aren't vibrating in many realities at the *same time*? Our attention is usually on *this* life. So much is going on all the time right *now*, that we choose to keep our awareness centered on one lifetime at a time.

Eckhart Tolle tells us that there is only the *now*. The past cannot be altered in anything but *now*; the future cannot be changed—we can change the way we do things which will change things "in the future"—but it all has to happen in the present.

I have discovered, however, that the clients whose past life experiences have been revealed to them through me, or through other resources, have benefitted greatly.

The soul knows about all its *lifetimes* and keeps track of all that happens in the outer experience of life. It knows what it wants or needs to experience. Perhaps it has a mission in this lifetime.

People ask me if I am on a spiritual path. I have to laugh now. What is a spiritual path? This heart, this mind, this body, the ground it is standing upon—it is all God! How about thoughts, positive or negative ones—it is all God! There is no separation, no division between God and man, only what we perceive it to be. We choose duality out of psychological need, of distancing, or non-acceptance, or denial of who we really are. Individual persons we may perceive as separate, but in truth we are all One, One energy that is used by all, vibrating at unique levels.

Using our natural psychic ability is merely training our awareness to block or move extraneous information aside in order to see, hear or feel what we or the person with whom we are working needs to know or experience. So, without judgement, as instruments or mediums of information, when we can zero in on the vibrations and listen to the messages contained therein, we are tapping into Energy, somewhat like a computer accessing memory.

The information just flows from me out to the client from the non-ending pool of Energy that is opened to me.

It is all Energy. It is all Good. And It is what I chose to call God.

2

Mentors Along the Way of Life

When we first become conscious of our own extra-sensory perception it appears to be out of the blue, a sudden realization. However, I believe that a breakthrough occurs when the soul is ready to express these gifts through the personality. Each individual will react in a different way. Some will view it in fear, some in awe and wonder, and some with gratefulness. And this reaction comes from knowledge—or lack of it—about metaphysical matters.

It is there all the time, waiting to be discovered and implemented. When we feel, hear or see it, and acknowledge it, for the first time, we are "blown away." It is actually our soul's deep desire to bring this knowledge to the conscious mind.

Unconsciously, we start using our psychic abilities at the first breath out of our mother's womb. Consciously, it may be many earth years before we pay attention, question it, then start to cultivate it.

Some people are frightened by the seemingly abrupt glimpse into a world of the unknown and never consciously seek it. Others are cautioned against looking any further by well meaning people.

Usually as children, before we acquire filters or judgements, our psychic gifts are accepted as natural extensions to our other obvious senses. Psychic occurrences are often called coincidences by most of our society. In recent years however these phenomena have been accepted more readily.

Those who shape our lives do not always come in the form of people who "have all the answers." No. Even seemingly negative persons form patterns that cling to our psyche and may even have a positive effect. They certainly have a learning effect on us.

Everything that we experience has a meaning. Our experiences shape our personalities of course, and they also have a tremendous impact on our psychic abilities. As fast as we can comprehend them, lessons are attracted into our day-to-day lives, some of which are rapidly learned and remembered. Others sit in our consciousness perhaps for years before we unconsciously get them out, dust them off and use them. These instances are met with our question, "How did I know that?"

I learned a lot from my parents and early teachers. I was an observer, you see, and so inquisitive. When I was about five years old I heard my name being called by an unknown voice over a period of several days. I looked for the source in vain. Finally, frustrated and annoyed, I answered, "What do you want?"

The voice stopped nagging me, but I felt that it had gotten what it wanted—my attention. I realize now that it was an opening of the gift of clairaudience.

Later, I began to wonder why I knew without being told that my aunt was coming for a visit hours or days before her arrival and was always dressed and ready to receive her when she came. My mother used to say, "Where are you going all dressed up?" No surprise to me, my aunt would appear at our door minutes or hours later. (See Chapter on Gifts)

I would go to the mailbox *knowing* that there was a letter therein from relatives at a distance. I didn't think there was anything strange or unusual about it.

On one occasion, my mother had applied for citizenship and had been anxiously awaiting the acceptance papers for weeks. She would go to the post office two miles from home just to be frustrated another day.

One day I awoke and said to her, "Today is the day when your citizenship papers will arrive!" Sure enough, the note was in the box instructing her to go to the nearest post office to pick up a registered letter.

I was using clairsentience, but I would not know that there was a name for it until many years later.

When I asked my parents or teachers how I could have known these things, the answer was always, "just a lucky guess," or "a fluke." Coincidence?

I spent my formative years in a Pennsylvania coal mining town, called a "patch." Patches were substandard developments built to house miners and their families. They were adequate, comfortable houses just alike and all the fathers worked in the mines.

With my father being a periodic alcoholic and my mother having psychotic breaks every year at the same time—from the end of January through February—my childhood upbringing was constant chaos. I lived with the belief that turmoil in one's life was natural.

When I began to predict accidents in the local mine with uncanny accuracy, I was threatened by my mother not to tell anyone. My mother was alarmingly afraid of superstition and the narrow-mindedness of our neighbors and church members. When she was a girl her Czechoslovakian mother babbled about people riding in flying buses before they were a reality. She was familiar with elf-like creatures with which she communicated. At that time, people ridiculed her family because they thought her mother was insane.

There is a difference between being *psycho* and *psychic*, but in our early history there was no distinction. People who foretold the future were called witches and were put in chains, or at the very worst, burned at the stake.

The Holy Bible:

Being of Czechoslovakian descent, we were Catholic and kept the traditions. My earliest collections are of mass on Sunday mornings and the smells of the huge dinners that followed. It was the custom in my school to have the Bible read each morning. These readings came to be a highlight of my early school years as they left me feeling uplifted and fascinated and I wanted to hear more. Having a Bible of my very own became an obsession. How and where did I get one? There were no stores in town that sold Bibles.

Early one Sunday morning before mass I gathered up enough courage to ask our stoic priest where a Bible such as they used in school could be purchased. He made light of the intensity of my longing by telling my mother and I that it could only be bought in Pittsburgh. He said this as if it were 500 miles away, when in fact it was more like 50 miles. He further declared that it was very, very far away and unthinkable that anyone would even consider going out of his way to satisfy the mere desires of an eight year old child.

This incident stands out as one of the major disappointments in my childhood. To think that my mother and father accepted the priest's words without question and that the priest, who represented the Catholic Church and the nearest thing they would ever get to the Pope, had so little compassion for the spiritual yearnings of a child baffled me. If I were not going to learn from the priest, if I were not going to trust the principles and values of my parents, then the Bible was the answer for me.

This was a turning point in my religious exposure and from that moment on I began to search for a religion that I could understand. I never did get a Bible of my own while I lived at home but I discovered that the school library had a Bible in the reference section. I continued to go through the motions of going to mass on Sundays but I never did really accept all that our priest told us in his sermons. I always had questions that were never answered to my satisfaction.

During one of those Sunday mornings as I fidgeted in the fourth or fifth row, I went against my training and turned around to look for a friend. I began to notice that there were lights of tremendous depth and color surrounding many of the parishioners—some very bright and vivid, while others were muddy and grey. I nudged my mother and started to ask her to clarify what I was seeing. She "hushed me" for talking in church and physically turned me around to face the front. By the time mass was over there were other things taking precedence over my thoughts, but from then on when I thought about that day I looked for lights in everyone I met.

I spoke to the priest of our parish one day about the "lights" around the heads of some of the parishioners. From the look I got, you would have thought I had suddenly grown antlers! I learned much later to refer to these lights as "auras."

My ignorant leaders and my fearful mother taught me to believe that there was something very wrong with me, so I kept further incidents to myself. I feared that whatever my mother was possessed with during her episodes of crying, shouting and irrational behavior, might be passed on to me. It was years before I dared to share my experiences with anyone. I learned to "stuff" my gifts into the back of my mind where they stayed ignored for much of my teenage and young adult years.

3

The Instrument Opens

After I had been married and divorced twice and just beginning my thirties I met a person who was familiar with psychic phenomena. She became my first teacher. Her name was Carol. She talked about having poltergeists in her home. I had never read any books on the supernatural, psychics or metaphysics and was unfamiliar with the terminology. She seemed familiar with the paranormal so hesitatingly I told her that I had been feeling a presence in my bathroom and admitted my fears about things of this nature.

To my surprise, she validated my experience and was eager to pursue it further. I just wanted it all to go away. I didn't know then that this was to change my perception of life and my purpose in it.

Carol forced me to confront my fear head on. Together we went into my bathroom and I had an incident that forever shut the door on unbelief and opened an awareness of my psychic senses.

Carol sat on the toilet seat facing the open doorway, while I stood at the sink. I turned on the water and looked in the mirror at the open doorway. Nothing happened for quite a while and then I began to feel goose bumps all over my body. I sensed that something had entered the room and was behind me.

"What is it?" Carol said, noting my apprehensive look.

"I don't know!" I whispered, gesturing behind me with my thumb. "Something is there. Tell me what to do!"

Her eyes filled with tears as she said, "Rosemarie, I can't see anything. I have no idea what you should do now. It's your experience. I've never felt or seen anything like that, but I know it is all good."

"I can't!"

"Yes, you can!" She said through her sobs. "It's a beautiful thing. I know it will be all right. I feel good about it. There is nothing to fear here."

I took a deep breath and spun around. I saw a transparent figure in the doorway. It was like an outlined shroud. I could see the form and the wall behind it. Quickly, I whirled back and began describing it to Carol. All of a sudden there was a large puff of smoke-like substance that materialized and surrounded my body, forming "fingers" in front of me. These "fingers" turned and went into my solar plexus area and I felt like a sponge absorbing energy. As the ethereal substance entered my body I experienced every good thing that had ever occurred in my life. Although I was not in full awareness, I entered another level of energy. When it was over I was so overwhelmed that I turned to Carol and said, "You have to go home now."

I was thinking that this was the beginning of a psychotic breaks like my mother had for so many years. I didn't want anyone to see me like that.

As I walked Carol to the front door she grabbed my arm. Her eyes were still watery when she said, "Rosemarie, please. You have to go to a psychic, somebody who knows all about these things."

"Okay. Okay." But I thought: no, tomorrow I'm making an appointment with a shrink. I have definitely cracked.

I went to bed that night still puzzled, but in a euphoric state. I felt a deep peace, a peace I had never before known. For many days afterwards I walked around in a happy daze, noticing everything looked sharper, more alive and had more meaning than ever before. My connection with my children changed drastically. With absolute clarity and for the first time I *heard* my kids; I noticed their body language, I felt their feelings, and I acknowledged everything in a new way. My perceptions and inner knowing changed forever. A deep compassion was birthed in me.

In a book by Wayne Dyer called, *There is a Spiritual Solution to Every Problem,* the book that I felt I co-authored with him, Dr. Dyer talks about energy and levels of vibration. At the level of everyday human consciousness we deal with illness and a feeling of separateness. He says, "… there is only one problem that we face, and that is our belief that we are separate from God. As you increase the frequency at which you live, you shift your energy field to a level wherein you elicit the qualities of Godliness. You become pure spirit. You see no divisions and you know that you are connected to everyone and all living creatures … you literally see the unfolding of God in every flower, creature and person."

I believe that I had touched upon what Dr. Dyer was talking about.

I wish I could say that this peace lasted, but life's challenges and lessons continued. I was still raising a handicapped son and two daughters by myself, working and trying to keep up with mountains of laundry and bills. However, that incident forever shut the door on my skepticism and opened my awareness and acceptance of my psychic senses.

I have not stopped learning and experiencing since that evening.

Carol, a seeker herself, hounded me until I agreed to see a known psychic for clarification of just exactly what it all meant.

4

Seeing a Psychic

And so it was that I went reluctantly to the psychic. I wasn't sure what a psychic was, although I had a picture in my mind of a gypsy woman wearing colorful jewelry and outrageous clothing who sat at a round table with a crystal ball in the center.

The woman's name was Dorothy—that's certainly an ordinary name for a psychic, I thought. Shouldn't it be "Madame Slabornowsky," or something?

Timidly, I pressed the doorbell and stood back, ready to bolt!

"Come!" someone yelled impatiently from within.

I gingerly opened the door and stepped inside.

"Come!" the voice repeated and I followed it.

When I entered the tiny room I saw a small table and two chairs and a couch against one wall. Seated there was a shriveled woman with large, piercing eyes, looking all of ninety years old and clearly irritated.

Without introduction, not even a greeting or a comment about the weather, she said in a demanding tone, "Well, how did you get this to happen?"

I hadn't yet told her why I was there.

I managed to croak, "Wha … Uh. I don't know."

She indicated a spot on the couch next to her and I sat.

"How much meditation do you do?" she asked in the same accusatory tone.

"Meditation? I don't really know what that is."

Dorothy reached for a Bible and thrust it toward me. "Do you know the story of Paul in the Bible?"

"Well, I know who Paul was."

"Do you know what happened to him on his travel to Damascus?"

"I'm not sure ..."

"I think you'd better read the story," she barked.

I felt like a ten year old being confronted by an angry teacher.

Meekly I promised, "Okay. I will."

Seemingly satisfied, she launched into a psychic reading for the next hour. She told me I was going to have another child and it would be a girl. Well, since I had had some female surgery and the doctor told me I had a 5-10 percent chance of getting pregnant, I was seriously doubtful.

She told me my brother and grandfather were very happy where they were; at that time they had both passed into the next life, out of body.

She said that I was going to quit my job, that I was going to be doing what she was doing on a larger scale and that I would be in the public eye. I thought she was really crazy! In fact, just about everything she said I refuted in my mind. Afterwards, I politely thanked her and left. I never went back.

Many years later, I discovered that this psychic was the grandmother of my second daughter's husband! How we do come together time and time again!

At the time I was not aware that the woman had given me a five year reading. Looking back I recognize that it was a dramatic, altering point in my life.

But I went blithely on, working and taking care of my children.

Life works in mysterious ways. Before two years had passed I had married again and had given birth to a beautiful red haired daughter. I was swamped with work, having believed that I had to be a supermom. The baby was still in diapers when my neighbor, Shirley saw me in the yard one day and ran over to talk with me.

She said, “I just heard of a fantastic psychic who is going to be at the metaphysical church I attend. Would you like to go with me to hear her?”

Thinking fast, I said, “I don’t have time. I’m ironing tonight. Besides, I don’t really want to go hear a psychic. Is that like a medium?”

“Well, yes!”

“No. I don’t want to go. I went to a psychic and everything she said was wrong.” And then it dawned on me that up until that time at least two of the things she told me had happened. Later that day I decided that I would get a sitter and go.

5

Becoming Aware

Psychometry

I reluctantly went to a metaphysical church with my friend. We drew door prize stubs and after about thirty minutes a woman named Joan was introduced. They began calling numbers. She went into a trance-like state and told each of the winners different things about themselves. I thought the whole thing was a waste of money.

Then my number was called and I stood up. She began to relate the very same things that Dorothy had said two years before!

I said to myself, "No way! I have enough to do raising my children. I don't want to be a *psychic* or *trans-medium* or any other crazy thing. I just want to remain who I am and be a housewife and mother."

I was a little angry and disappointed. When we were driving home Shirley, my friend and neighbor, told me that the church had psychic development classes and wanted to know if I would like to join her in taking a course or two. My head said, "No—definitely, no!"

After much persuasion, I let Shirley talk me into going to the first meeting so that she wouldn't have to go alone. I was curious to see if it was anything I could use to help me. I certainly didn't expect what happened that first night!

As we entered the meeting I noticed that there was a coffee table upon which was piled rings, watches and other jewelry. Before I could figure out what that was about, the minister, who turned out to be Joan's husband, said, "Please take off an article and place it on the table here."

Shirley was in the process of taking off her watch, so I slipped a ring off and dropped it on the table. There were about 10 people in the room, seated in an oval configuration. Joan was at one end; the minister at the other end.

We were instructed to focus our attention on our third eye—what was that?

Noticing that I had a blank expression, the minister pointed to the middle of his forehead and gestured for me to close my eyes. We were asked to silently say our favorite prayer. Mine was, and is, the Prayer of St. Francis.

"Would you please start?" said the minister, indicating the person at his left, which happened to be me.

When he saw the puzzled look, he asked, "Is this your first time?"

Was this my first time for what? I thought, but nodded sheepishly.

"Okay then. Pick up an article that is not your own and hold it on your third eye."

I slinked down on my knees and picked up a woman's watch, which I held on my forehead, and turned around to get further instructions.

"Close your eyes and take a couple of deep breaths and relax. Then give off whatever may come to you." Give off? Oh, sure!

As soon as I closed my eyes and before I exhaled, something clicked off and something else clicked on. A picture began to unfold and I started describing what I saw, heard and felt. Although I don't know what I said, I went on for about fifteen minutes. I finished and put the watch down.

The room was silent with all eyes on me! I was not afraid but was I ever embarrassed!

The accuracy of what I had related was confirmed by the owner of the watch.

Joan said, "Have you ever done this before?"

"No," said I, cowering in my seat.

She took hold of me and, drawing me into the kitchen of their home, said, "You are naturally clairvoyant!"

While I was wondering what that was and trying to outline a plan to escape as soon as possible, she made some tea. We sipped the tea and she launched into an explanation of clairvoyance and psychometry, which is what I had just done. It was as if a veil had lifted. My fears of becoming psychotic that I had held onto for years were finally being dispelled. This was sort of fun!

After that experience I couldn't shut off the pictures in my head, nor the feelings I had. It was like I was getting all worlds at one time and I had no idea how to stop them from coming at me. I called Joan in panic frequently in desperation due to almost daily paranormal happenings. I had many questions.

Joan became my first mentor; she helped me to understand my natural gifts and how to use them. For several years I stayed with Joan and the church that she and her husband formed. I began to read and research numerous metaphysical writers. I really enjoyed gathering information, some of which I agreed with and not at all with others. Our individual truth?

In several months' time I became a professional psychic reader and worked at the church. When I began charging for my sessions I had a difficult time with the concept. I felt that I should be giving readings freely, because my gifts had been given to me freely. I got straightened out on that one when someone reminded me that a teacher passes his gift onto others, but charges for lessons.

The phone rang constantly with individuals wanting questions answered. Then one morning a person was sitting on my front porch wanting a session.

Becoming professional was a necessity—definite client hours, fees and learning professional behavior.

I believe that we are teachers, students and lovers in every relationship we have. We may not recognize what role we are playing at the time, but with reflection and understanding this becomes clear to us. Do we learn from these experiences? I certainly hope we do!

6

Desires of the Soul

We come into this physical experience with a deep soul yearning. Some of us bury these desires in a corner of our consciousness, never to crop up again in this lifetime. The universe would not let me do that. My life's experiences seemed to bring them into awareness and force me to move on in my spiritual path, whether or not I thought I was ready.

When the father of my fourth child left me I was devastated, not because he had gone–we were never real soul mates and our marriage had been fraught with problems–but because I had no means of support for my four children. When I look back on my separation and divorce I can truly say that my ex-husband had been one of my greatest teachers, but at the time I was lost and defeated.

At the time I was not aware that the severity of emotional reactions was a "red flag" pointing to our lesson concerning a particular incident. Instead of reacting emotionally, and thus erratically, stop right there! Ask yourself, "Where does this pain come from?" Remember, the lesson that it signifies could be coming from this lifetime, or one previously lived.

I had been doing psychic readings at the church and earned some money, but it just didn't feel right. I had to concentrate on making a life for my children and myself.

I had to make a decision to either get a job or leave the church and start giving readings on my own. I began to listen to the guidance of my soul.

Around that time, a professional friend asked me if I would be interested in taking a position as a clairvoyant at an exclusive health spa. I would do psychometry just as I did the first time I used it—the very first time I went to the meeting at Joan's house.

I work in much the same way today, however, through the years I have acquired more trust in those available to assist me both in and out of body. I shut down my active self with deep breathing and concentration on the metal object that is given to me and when I am "in the vibrations" of the client, the words just tumble out of my mouth. I do not always "hear" what I am saying; I just let the energy flow through me and say whatever is for the client to hear.

Later while I was doing a series of lectures aboard a popular cruise ship, a private client said, "You don't really need to hold the object anymore." He was right. Since then, I call out the client's name, breathe, wait patiently, and the doors to the universe open.

It frightened me just a little in that early stage of development to branch out into the "real world" and have celebrities come to me for information to solve their dilemmas ... I was eager to do it! However I felt that I had a lot of obstacles to overcome.

The opportunity to work at the health spa would mean money to help me with my household expenses and raise my kids. Everything fell into place: I called Joan at the church and she encouraged me to do it. I had a car that was in good running order and my Mother was happy to be with my children from Thursday through Sunday nights.

I went timidly, but determinedly, into unchartered territory. My confidence grew as I progressed. I gave readings for celebrities in the film industry and dignitaries from government and business. Before long I had a substantial following and was booked solidly each weekend. This lasted about two years and gave a broader field to my professional, as well as my personal life. And, I was having fun doing it!

My psychic experiences accelerated at a rapid rate. Everything began happening at once!

One rainy morning I was fixing breakfast and had the children's dishes all lined up on the kitchen counter. All at once I heard a rattling sound and saw the bowls scooting across the counter all by themselves.

At first it frightened me, so after settling the kids at the table I called Joan at her home.

"What does it mean when inanimate things move on their own?" I demanded to know!

Joan calmly said, "Rosemarie, I feel that someone is trying to tell you something. Just get quiet and mentally ask what it could mean. Call me later."

So, I went into my bedroom, sat down on the bed and breathed deeply until I felt relaxed and receptive. I asked my question and waited for a reply. I got the feeling that I was to caution my daughter Tonette, who was about 6 or 7 years old, to be extra careful crossing the street that day, to look both ways before stepping off the curb.

I got the children ready for school and gave my warning about crossing the street before they left the house. Some time later Tonette was at the backdoor, soaking wet and calling for me. She told me that a car had splashed water all over her and came very close to her. She said that if she had not done as I had told her the car would have hit her!

Paying attention to that paranormal activity, listening to that inner voice and acting on its advice had virtually saved her life!

Several days later I was getting ready for a meeting that Joan had scheduled at my house on past life regression. I had worked all morning and was putting Terri into her crib for a nap when I began to hear music from an old organ we had been given. It was the type of organ that needed to be turned on and warmed up for a few minutes before it was operational. I knew that the organ playing was physically impossible, as well as downright scary. I couldn't wait until I confronted the person who was in my house. At the time I thought perhaps a friend had come in, saw the organ and decided to play it. Of course, when I went into the living room, I saw that there was no one there and the organ was turned off!

By this time I was fairly used to psychic phenomena occurring at odd times and didn't put any great stock in it. I did, however, wonder why it couldn't just leave me alone. I thought if I just ignored it, it would go away. It was at this time I made an inner decision and actually stated it: unless this phenomena served a purpose for myself or others, I would not accept just "phenomena!"

I truly believe that at some deep level we choose to become instruments. The Universe just waits until we begin to pay attention to the signs and symbols, then when we acknowledge them, all stops are pulled out. There were days when I could keep things at bay, but it was a struggle. When I began to work with them I found that my predictions never faltered. I was not the only one who was amazed and sometimes shaken with the accuracy. My regular clients and the people with whom I worked at the Spa were constantly calling me to say that what I told them had come true. Just when I was about to chuck the whole thing and go find a *real* job was when I realized that I was actually helping people with their lives.

Getting out of our own developed personality's way and following the desires of the soul may only take one time, but with trust and the willingness to listen to your soul, you will be guided.

Did I want to turn my back on this? I was finally doing something in my life that I could be proud of—but could I make a living doing it?

The next couple of months were spent experimenting with different ways of receiving and learning about my psychic gifts.

Joan had her meeting on past life regression at my place. She used me as a subject for study. Not ever having remembered a life before this one, I was skeptical but willing to learn.

Joan was a licensed hypnotherapist. After putting me into a trance-like state I was regressed to a life that I had experienced many, many lifetimes ago. That lifetime had begun in Norway and ended in America. I related the story in detail. It was months later that that story was brought to full circle. (See Chapter on Past Life)

Someone told me about automatic writing; I wasn't sure how that worked, but I wanted to try it for myself. Early morning was the best time for me to be quiet and concentrate. I was told that all you did was have paper ready and hold a pen or pencil in your hand, do some deep breathing to center yourself, and let the words write themselves.

Well, I wasn't at all prepared for what happened! Suddenly, it felt like someone much bigger than I occupied my body and the pen took off on its own. I wrote deep, philosophical things that I barely understood then. It was only after studying philosophy, religion and psychology that I could comprehend what I had written.

I had been sitting at the kitchen table letting my pen write for several mornings when my daughter and her friend, who had spent the night, came into the kitchen where I was writing. They were anxious to get to school that day and had gotten up earlier than usual. I explained what I was doing and how it seemed to happen. My daughter's friend had just lost her father and she asked me if he could communicate through me. I told her that I didn't know, but that I would concentrate on him next time I sat down to write and let her know if I had any success.

Remember, I was still a novice at this energy business and very willing to investigate everything at my disposal. And, if it helped someone, I was more than willing to do it.

After directing my thoughts on Candy's father whom I had known just slightly I wrote the following:

Hello. At this time we have the person here. He is well. Tell her he sends love and joy—no suffering involved, nor any loneliness, this is sure. One may believe in the right path. All is well. This will answer the questions: Tell her about the shoe. It is in the car in the garage. Tell her the end is not the end. There will be many messengers among you …

I was flabbergasted! I couldn't wait to give her this message.

At first there was no shoe. Then, within that month Candy called from a gas station. Her mother was having a flat tire fixed. Wedged under the spare in a tire well, there it was … her dad's golf shoe! (See section on Automatic Writing)

Just when I thought that I discovered all there was to know about psychism and the connection we have with everything in the universe, including what we think of as the "departed," something else would open to me.

While the automatic writing was going on, a call came from the local YMCA asking if I would like to teach a class on extra sensory perception. So I said, "of course," not knowing what I would teach. I sat down at my kitchen table with fresh paper and a pen, settled myself into another level of consciousness, and an eight week class was outlined.

It was there at the Y that another one of my earth teachers came into my life. Her name was Martha. She had studied with many well known metaphysical and philosophical individuals and entertained them at her home. She was a blessing to me. She was instrumental in opening my psychic senses to the fullest degree, avenues that I would never have traveled or experienced.

She and her husband were doing some experimentation in trance channeling and wanted to talk to me about it. I knew very little about the subject but was quite curious so I scheduled a visit to their home at a later date.

That visit began weekly sessions. I would arrive and Martha would assist me to go to deeper levels of trance. I don't remember much of anything that I said. It was as if I, or my personality, moved out of the way so that the information could come through. The sessions were taped. It was during these sittings that an entity came through called Bartholomew who announced that he was the keeper of the gate and that communication would come from him. I had heard from "Bartholomew" in my automatic writings, so I wasn't surprised when Martha told me about meeting him through me.

In the next months the trance work became very profound. I listened to the tapes and was amazed at what had been said with my voice. (See Trance Work, Part II, Chapter 4.)

Just when I thought that "I knew it all," someone else would call me to book a session, or give a talk or ask me if I had heard of "so-and-so's" new book. I was exposed to many books. Some of it I accepted;

some I rejected. That's the way I believe people might read, from their individual truth.

The multiple psychic experiences continued. No longer afraid of the contact, it was like a gap in the connecting thread between in-the-body and out-of-body personalities, touching on higher vibrations of energy where communication was possible. I was deluged with visitations and activities. And, thankfully my practice began to expand. My life was full and fulfilling. I knew that I was finally doing something that I was born to do. Every time I felt that it was *me* who was doing this work I was brought back sharply, and I now will never forget that the material comes through me.

PART II

TOOLS OF THE SPIRIT

1

Natural Gifts of the Spirit

The Bible refers to talents and gifts that were given to us from creation: *"Having then gifts differing according to the grace that is given to us, whether prophecy ... Or ministry ... or he that teacheth ... let him do it with simplicity ... "* (Romans 12:6)

I believe that some of these gifts are extra-sensory and have always been part of the human being. That we don't use all of our talents is an outgrowth of our programming. If everyone exercised these talents, just as a pianist or painter practices his gift, all beings would be seers and tellers of Truth. Who knows, the world may be a more peaceful and beautiful place, an Eden much like that which was created for us.

All of us have had intuitions and "hunches," especially while we were growing up and taking everything into our experience. Sadly, most of us have pushed talents down into our consciousness where they lie virtually unused.

Another quote from the Bible tells us that these gifts should be shared for a very important benefit: "*For ye may all prophesy one by one, that all may learn, and all may be comforted.*"(I Corinthians 14:31).

In extra-sensory perception there are three basic receptors that define all the talents given to us for prophecy. They are clairvoyance, clairaudience and clairsentience. In very much the same way that our memory stores information, our minds categorize things in an individual, unique manner to each of us, either sight, sound or movement (smell, touch, sense).

CLAIRVOYANCE

Clairvoyance is the gift of an ability to "see" things that are not immediately apparent to the eye. A clairvoyant is described as someone who has extra sensory perception and is able to look into things that are not present to the ordinary senses.

Children have imaginary friends that are just as real to them as their corporeal friends. Whether they are brought forward into existence from their imaginations, or whether they are entities from the spirit world, they are usually seen, heard or interacted with.

CLAIRAUDIENCE

The meaning of clairaudience is much the same as the meaning for clairvoyance in that sound, or words, rather than pictures, are heard by the psychic "ear" without physical proof.

This phenomenon came first and was my introduction to what is known as the paranormal. I heard my name being called and when I acknowledged it, it was as if something were testing me and that part of my psychic awareness was then proven to it, so it went on to other senses.

Hearing is the first sense that a baby has that connects with the human experience. It is the last sense that a dying person uses to hold onto the physical world.

Have you ever been all alone and heard a sound, or a word, that frightened you into stopping what you were doing, or at the least slowed you down? Then, later you realized that if you had continued, something unpleasant might have happened?

Some people have only this specific gift—the gift of psychic hearing—however I believe that all of the psychic senses can be developed and fine tuned when the connection to the one energy is opened fully.

CLAIRSENTIENCE

This is of the ability to sense or feel, smell or taste, that is not physically evident. Grouped together with this gift is the "knowing" without being informed.

We have all smelled a familiar scent that reminded us of someone dear to us, only to realize that person was not near. Or perhaps we feel a presence close by and turn to greet them, only to discover no one standing there.

A knowing that a certain event was imminent, even though proof of it was not apparent, is another form of clairsentience.

These signs of the psychic are not always recognized as warnings or portends of things to come. We tend to brush off one of its occurrences as coincidence. Have you ever been thinking of someone very strongly for a few hours, or days, and "out of the blue" that person calls, or pops up?

When I heard my name being called, day after day, it was more annoying than anything else. At my five years I had no fear of things like this. It certainly wasn't anything out of the ordinary to question, or cause me to be frightened. When I finally shouted, "What? What do you want?" into the air, there was no response. At least no auditory one.

To discover which gift of the senses is your strongest, try the following experiment. This will involve the practice of psychometry, so be sure that you have a piece of metal from your subject and of course, the person's permission to use it:

Sit in a quiet place. Uncross your arms or legs; plant your feet on the floor and arms at your side, or hands resting on your lap. Hold the metal item in your hand and close your eyes. It may take a few minutes of meditation before you notice anything. You may get something right away.

Don't force it. If you begin to see pictures, symbols or shapes, your strong gift is *clairvoyance*. If you hear words or sounds, it is *clairaudi-*

ence. If feelings, or sometimes smells, are experienced, you have *clairsentience.* Practice is what makes the gift stronger.

TELEPATHY

Telepathy is the communication of one mind with another without direct contact. This can be conscious or unconscious. We have all had experiences with people who unexpectedly pop into our minds with a thought or event. I believe that since we are all connected in mind, we are "broadcasting" our thoughts or fears all the time. Those who pick up these things are said to be telepathic.

"Tele" means distant; "pathy" denotes feelings. This is an accepted human ability in the field of psychism. It is theatrically called, "reading minds."

Freud thought that it was a regressed sexuality that had become discarded as it was not reliable. Some of his patients spoke about it in psychological sessions. He gave the ability no credence.

Some scholars have written that telepathy was the first real communication of our very early ancestors when direct access was not available. Perhaps they were right. Even today in jungles of Africa there is silent communication between members of a tribe. It keeps the members informed of what is happening.

Telepathy can be a very conscious type of communication. Our military have experimented with "remote viewing" with relative success. It is done by someone sitting in a room and either looking at, or thinking about, something specific.

For instance, person A looks at a shape or a picture and concentrates his attention, while person B in a different room, or across continents, tries to "receive" the shape or picture, by inner sight, sound or feeling. This is done repeatedly using flash cards. The reception is monitored and compared to the items *sent* and the number of *hits* are recorded. The accuracy varies, but with practice, the results tend to improve remarkably.

In an ION's (Institute of Noetic Sciences) article about space travel, it was reported that NASA (National Aeronautical Space Administration) conducted an experiment during a space mission with Astronaut Edgar Mitchell. He concentrated on a series of numbers, while a receiver on earth wrote down what he saw or felt. Out of over two hundred sequences, almost half were *hits.*

Metaphysical psychologist Lawrence LeShan, who wrote a book about meditation techniques, suggested that each person was gifted with his own reality and some used this phenomenon of telepathy, or remote viewing, with regularity.

Studies with twins have touched on the likelihood of telepathy between the two individuals. Pets have shown this gift with their owners.

In times of great stress or danger to a friend, messages can be telepathically received. Most of us have gotten a feeling that something was wrong, called the person involved and found that person had been reaching out due to a problem in his life.

TELEKINESIS

I haven't had much experience with *telekinesis*, but I have seen it demonstrated many times. It is the ability to move an object without touching it. It also defines the changing of shape in a metal object.

There was a great deal of interest in this gift several years after I had gotten into the paranormal. People practiced this gift by attempting to bend metal objects, such as spoons. Also, moving small objects from one side of a table to another. It is done with the power of concentration and belief that it can happen.

There are articles on the internet that teach the process of telekinesis.

With the acceptance of other avenues of communication, all sorts of things began to happen. In my innocence I gathered everything into my knowledge of life and what it was all about. I had been stifled at an early age when the priest at the church our family attended admonished me about religious observance, coupled with my mother's fear of anything that smacked of the supernatural. I suppressed any further divulgence of precognitive or other worldly occurrences.

Much, much later as an adult I again began to pay attention and to act on my clairvoyance, clairaudience, and clairsentience. Luckily, this happened before these talents were lost. Otherwise, I wouldn't be sharing my experiences by writing this book.

Ancient writings speak of healing talents. I have witnessed many healings in my work throughout the years. This is one of the most important facets of the so called paranormal, the ability to heal. Of course, we in the physical body do not heal anything. We merely call attention to the perfection and direct the energy. (Please see the Chapter on Healing further in this book.)

Check out your gifts. Pay attention to incidents that are out of the ordinary. Look for confirmation of them in the following minutes, days, or weeks. You are psychic! Believe it!

When I was young and experiencing the life of a single mother with two children, one of whom was handicapped and required numerous surgeries to keep him alive and functioning, the last thing on my mind were psychic contacts, or anything other than work and children. But I soon discovered Spirit had other plans for me.

2

Meditation: Connecting with the Source

It is said that prayer is talking to God. Meditation, then, can be said as listening to God, or the Source, opening your receptivity to the Universe in order to connect with the Energy—All that Is.

For most of us, thought is a purposeless stream of consciousness, somewhat like an uncut motion picture film that plays our own confused (or enlightened) inner dialog simultaneously with the soundtrack. During the act of meditation, however, these undirected thought patterns are put on hold as conscious awareness vibrates toward another level.

Meaning wisdom, the word "meditation" comes from the Sanskrit word, "meta," and is the process by which we receive, or experience, the wisdom of God. A unique procedure of mind, it is characterized by suspension of outer concerns and claims our humblest attention. It is like listening with an empty mind; its basis is quietude and stillness.

In *The Joy of Meditation,* Jack and Cornelia Addington describe the process and purpose:

"Meditation is much like inviting God to enter us, or to speak to us, or to make Itself known to us … The purpose is to be still and let the awareness of God permeate us. There is no seeking after it; there is no striving for it. We begin with the realization: God is, God is where I am, I and the Father are one. In that realization you relax and invite the Father to reveal Itself; 'Speak, Lord, Thy servant heareth.' That is really the main function of meditation."

Today, there is vast research on the benefits of meditation and includes a variety of enterprises, from space exploration to the business world. Included in these we find that physiologists, psychologists and graduate students from Harvard to Stanford to Oxford have accumulated data on the effects of transcendental meditation on brainwave patterns, blood pressure, reaction time and metabolic efficiency. These groups now publish advice on how to design meditation experiments and what controls to employ.

Among those who contributed so much to the peoples of this world, Mahatma Gandhi and Albert Einstein often used meditation as a major process in decision making. Whether with friends or with political adversaries, Gandhi was often quoted saying, "Let's not hurry to a decision." He would then go into silence and meditate.

The benefits derived from meditation are numerous. In reference to the physiological positives, some say that the procedure creates a fourth state of consciousness, beyond waking, sleeping, and dreaming. The phrase, "A wakeful hypometabolic state," was coined by one group. Because this state of consciousness is the opposite in every way to the anxiety/alarm state we employ during most of our waking hours, it has the effect of regenerating energy by causing the awareness to accelerate to a heightened awareness.

Meditation has been known to influence physical health and wellbeing in cases of ulcers, allergies, asthma, epileptic seizures, depression, anxiety, arthritis, hypertension, heart conditions, etc. These physical and psychological improvements run throughout surveys of available literature on meditation. With meditation it is found that there exists a higher threshold for stress, development of deeper personal relationships, and happier attitudes. In terminal cases it has been known to affect fear of death, which seemed to fall off like an old cloak.

According to the Gospel of Buddha, there are five stages of meditation:

Meditation of Love. Readying the heart to love all beings, including enemies.

Meditation of Pity. Learning compassion for others.

Meditation of Joy. Thinking on the prosperity of others and rejoicing with them.

Meditation on Impurity. The consequences of negative thinking.

Meditation of Serenity. Rising above seeming opposites love/hate, wealth/lack and sitting in impartial calmness and perfect tranquility.

There are several ways that you may meditate. There is no wrong way, as long as it results in quieting the mind.

The method I use is simplistic, but effective for me. There are just a few simple steps. Choose a time period of ten to twenty minutes in an area where there will not be any distraction. As the process is learned you may choose to extend that time period. I always begin a psychic session with a meditation.

Sit in a comfortable chair with your feet flat on the floor and your hands in your lap. Begin breathing slowly and deeply through your nose, letting your stomach expand on inhalation as much as possible. Exhale slowly through your mouth while feeling the deflation of your stomach. With each breath, tell yourself through thoughts—not words aloud—to relax. Your eyes are closed as you begin to focus on a peaceful image, a single word or on your breathing. Allow your vision to focus at the center of your forehead where the third eye is said to be. This is done with your eyes remaining closed.

Breathe—relax—focus—let go. Repeat until it is done unconsciously. Enjoy your peaceful time where there are no responsibilities, no concerns, no interruptions.

Before long you may want to use meditation to help yourself, or another person, understand problems or complications that may arise. At the beginning of your meditation or when you find yourself in a receptive state, silently ask for guidance on a specific subject, or speak the name of the person you wish to help.

You may hear messages "inside your head" like words, sounds or music. This may very well be clairaudience. It may be instructions or answers to the questions you ask. (See Chapter on Symbolic Guidance)

It might be given in symbols that you "see" with your inner eye, somewhat like the images you experience in dreams. A feeling may come over you: peace, love, joy. Or, you might not experience anything at all, but do not be discouraged. Whether or not you have a revelation is not a measurement. *Something* always happens; a conscious connection with the Infinite is the opening of your awareness.

Just don't stop! Keep meditating every day. There is work that goes on in the silence whether or not our conscious mind is awake to receive it. To the degree that we are consciously aware of the Truth of our existence, it is brought into our experience. Full awareness of our higher Self, operating through our individuality, brings forth only that which is good, pure and true in our lives.

This greater knowledge can emerge through meditation. If we stay rooted in the effects of our lives, we will only experience those identical effects, time and time again. It is easy to get into that rut, believing that we are victims of outer manipulation, and we even say, "See, I told you everything bad happens to me!" It takes determination to break out of that groove. Changing your thoughts and actions does change your life. Believe it!

There are different types of meditation throughout the world and all depend upon "centering," or becoming single-focused. Don't wait for a break in your life "when you have time" or when disaster strikes. The sooner you begin, the sooner your life will change for the better.

3

One Life

In Paul's epistle to the Corinthians (II Corinthians 12.2) he talked about his experience on the road to Damascus, then twelve years earlier. He knew not at that time whether he had been in the body or out of the body. He said that there was no difference.

There is no separation between this existence and what some people call "The Other Side." There is just one Life in which we all live. It takes on many expressions and those manifestations are given free will. Whether they express in physical bodies or in ethereal, emotional or spiritual bodies is simply the form of which they consist at any given time.

I believe that we "stay with" other entities and incarnate with them. There are others who act as higher selves and guides from time to time who remain incorporeal. Based on research into this phenomenon, I have come to understand that while we are in a physical existence there is a nucleus of about 36 entities that enter into and out of our personal experience. Our families and extended families are part of the nucleus, but not limited to it. There are those who come into our lives that appear to create havoc for us, but in reality they either teach us, or they are students who learn from us.

Voices and Forms Beyond Physical Experience

If the universe is all energy, then it follows that the energy that is Uncle Joe remains, even when that personality "dies." His energy is incorporated into the soul, along with all of his other expressions of Life.

A few years after my father passed into his next expression I had gotten up during the night. Returning to my bed, my body seemed to detach itself: one got into bed, while the other—an ethereal body—stayed at the bedside. My father appeared next to me. I said, "What are you doing here? You are dead!" I took hold of his arm and squeezed. It felt like flesh and blood.

He returned my comment with a chuckle. He looked over my shoulder and said, "There are two others … within a year." Before I could ask what he meant, he vanished from physical sight. As he had related to me, within a year I had lost my long time dear friend and my favorite aunt. I learned to pay attention to these paranormal, dreamlike episodes.

On another occasion after a particularly difficult time, I awoke to see my deceased brother standing at the foot of my bed. I asked him, "Dempsey? Why are you here?" He had made his transition during the Korean Conflict, you see, and I was quite surprised to see him. He looked the same as when I had last seen him–some twenty years before.

He said, "I just dropped by to see you." I started to say, "but you are dead," when he laughed and in a puff, was gone.

Those two visits were to me proof that the afterlife indeed existed and that communication between this physical side and *that* side was a reality for me as I understood it.

Automatic Writing

Early in my psychic development I had come home from a meeting at the church and began thinking about what had been said about automatic writing. I was curious about what my experiments with it might bring forth. It seemed a simple procedure, a test in communication with those who had moved into a different experience. I was eager to try it.

So, fearing nothing, I began. I sat down at the kitchen table with a fresh piece of lined, 3-hole paper and pen in hand. I centered my consciousness and waited. I gripped the pen and waited. I closed my eyes and waited. Finally, I set the point of the pen down on the paper and just let go …

In a booming, masculine voice, I clairaudiently heard, "I am Bartholomew, your gatekeeper!" (My what? I was to learn that Bartholomew was one of my helpers, out of body, who played a major role in my professional life. In the years that passed we became great friends.)

"*I will permit only those in the light to pass through*!"

With that, my hand commenced to write:

Hello—at this time let me bring through a friend of your father's. This man will give you a message that will help them tell Mary to be careful when she is carrying a bucket of water. We see her tripping and a serious accident. Let this be known.

Now, there is one close to you who has a child, little; there will be for her a new home in the near future. Let this be known.

Much bustling here. Will move to a quieter location—there—there is no time for silly games.

My mind was boggling. I began to form inquiries for this person. I was having problems with a relationship with my daughter. My thoughts were interrupted with more scrawling:

What can you learn from those questions of such minor value. Let your questions be of sincerity and for the help of others. You can reach your daughter through patience and time alone with her. No one else present.

We are happy for more time. This is a pleasure and progress for us both. Do you understand?

Tell Libby her future is bright and colorful—Paris, Eiffel Tower. She will counsel many. After you have taken the course, so much more will be shown. Through God all is good. Find the right path and don't waver. God bless.

(The next my pen wrote boldly) *CHARLES KNIGHT!*

I took a big breath and sat back! Well, who was Charles Knight? I had never known anyone with that name.

When I read what I had written, I figured that the "Mary" he had written about was my mom. I called Pennsylvania and told her to be careful while carrying water.

The daughter that was mentioned was my daughter Pamela. She was a teenager at the time and I had difficulty communicating with her.

As far as "Libby" was concerned I knew no one with that name. It was several years later that I had a client called Libby. She gave me the opportunity to inspire her towards further education. She is now a professor of French, has studied in Paris, saw the Eiffel Tower and loved the experience. On many levels of energy "time" is not as we understand.

A few days later after my first successful experiment with automatic writing I was in the local library with a friend. There was a large book of biographies of famous persons laying open on a display table. As we entered, my eyes zeroed in on the name of one of the biographers, CHARLES KNIGHT!

Since the book was a reference-only copy I was unable to take it home, but you can bet that I returned several times in the next weeks to find out more about this person. I did further research and read that Charles Knight had worked with his father, who was a publisher. He collaborated on his father's version of the Bible. I was fascinated.

Bartholomew showed up several times in my automatic writing and as my guide in the trance sessions that came about several months later.

After it was proved that Charles had been a real person, the automatic writing continued with a flourish during the early development of my psychic abilities.

A particularly intriguing writing came in October of that year:

Let this be a sign to you. The cross is only as heavy as you make it to be. The only burden you have is releasing the soul to God for good, for service. You have been chosen to pass the word of God and you will not turn your back on this mission. These writings will mean much more later in time than they do at this period. We have faith in all God's children. We also realize your weaknesses. They are so many. (I considered myself properly chastised.)

Another writing that I think is important:

We here have been very patient in this matter of time that lapses and no writing is done. Man has much to learn. (All right!)

We now want for you a person of many assets who will begin to come into reality for you. Be sure this person is acknowledged properly. This means to assist him and not fight against him. Remember 1400, not 1800! (Was this referring to Bartholomew?) *This is important. The tale is the same even though interpretations are so different, lengthy and in detail.*

Now do you see the fox? ("Grey Fox" was the nickname of a man who had come into my life.) *Study him well at this time. He will never get lost for he will be lead by the Infinite. Charles will be seen shortly. Time will permit no chaos in the life of a true believer. Let God lead, guide and comfort. To be just is to be true to the inner self. How we learn now will go so much for—or against us. Let it be. Who amongst you deny Him denies life, all life, whether spiritual or physical. God denies no one, but he cannot come into closed doors. The lessons here must be learned.*

(There was a break here. Then:) *How the lost sheep trample over the stable ones. Pray for them for they are in such desperate need.*

Solomon was never a beggar, nor Bathsheba a slave, but they learned so well and came forward. We learn from observing but experience sets the lesson. June will come and brighten up all around the total environment. See the robin. Do unto others as you would have them do unto you. Pray for all. His glory is our goal. Hail God for all good. All is well. God Bless. CHARLES KNIGHT.

A day after the above:

Now is the time for unfolding knowledge learned through experience. This will be shown as we proceed further into development. Your guide is patiently waiting for acknowledgment. Do not cover, but let the lid come off with ease as this will produce the clearest picture.

I had to discover that I needed to move myself out of the way in order for the information to pour out. This took a lot of work as I was basically a Type A personality. A single mom with four children, one handicapped, what else could I have been? A controlling, fiercely-loving mother who would defend and protect to the death any of her brood, of course!

The classes that I have taught throughout the years on naturalness of psychism have shown me that anyone who has experienced the so-called supernatural can hone, or fine-tune, those gifts. Even those who merely came to the classes out of curiosity developed one form or the other of their natural psychic abilities. The recognition of One Life can only enhance our experience while in our present form.

Poltergeist Activity

From time to time I have had numerous evidences of poltergeists active in my home. One of my clients shared with me this story:

"Our two sons died in a car accident. For several months after their deaths they contacted people who could receive them to let us know that they were still 'alive.' Our experience was having things (coins, cigarette lighter, pictures, etc.) turn up in odd places where they could not have been left by us."

What was the purpose of this? Not only did my client feel that her sons had attempted to contact her, but the items she mentioned did appear in other places. This would prove that it is possible for discarnate entities to cause things to move around. What a way to get someone's attention!

4

Trance Work

Trance Work

Martha came to the very first class that I gave at the YMCA and surprised me with her knowledge and experience of metaphysics. She had read most of the available literature and sat with most of those prominent in matters referring to the supernatural for many years. She became my spiritual mentor the first few years of our relationship, a relationship that has lasted forty years.

The very first session that I had with Martha taught me that I could, with her help, push my conscious attention out of the way and concentrate on being a receptor, to just allow the words and pictures to come through without judgement or filter.

Martha had begun by saying, "We ask those beautiful forces about us right now to reach down as we reach up. We are trying to reach up and we know you are reaching down to our level. As we touch we ask sincerely that only those be present who are aware and in harmony with the Christ spirit. We release all entities and conditions that are not here in the spirit of the Christ.

"We bless them and dismiss them. We are here to offer this channel to those enlightened ones who are seeking a channel … When the time is right, use Rosemarie for her highest good and for the benefit of all humanity."

After about ten minutes, there was a sound that emanated from my mouth that sounded like, "Aieeyah!" A cry in the wilderness of consciousness that heralded the beginning of something deeper than I had ever before encountered.

Most of what was spoken through me I did not *hear* while the trance was in progress, but through the miracle of tape it is on record. From the recording of that initial encounter: (This is a direct tape quotation.)

"As we open up this evening, the very first symbol that we see is like a fleur de lis. It is the symbol that will be shown each time that we work in reference to the material that will be printed. It is a design that will be incorporated into the written material as a mark, or an opening, or a passage, or a door. This will be shown each time trance work begins."

This was the first indication that the work we were commencing was to be written down and printed. I didn't have the means to attempt to publish anything as far as I could see. The date on this first session was March 10, 1986. This was to lie in a box full of tapes for many years until a friend volunteered to transcribe the trance tapes for me. It was Legh, a gifted psychic who could take the spoken word and transfer it to paper.

To continue with that first encounter:

"The energies are being connected and it is those energies that have not been tapped for quite a long time. They appear like electrical wire ends that have rust on them. They need to be scraped and then sharpened and tied together. The connections are renewed and the cords are stronger than before."

Introduction to The Messengers

Rosemarie: "I am being taken to a large rock. There are five people standing around the rock, two on one side and three on the other."

"There will be a total of five questions. We will have assistance from ***each*** *one who is a specialist in his field. They will act as transmitters for the information to come through the instrument.*

"There is a very bright light on top of the boulder. It serves as an energy source for these five people so they can "build up" and we can talk with them."

These five people became my guides or helpers throughout my first years as a psychic counselor. Each of them was unique and presented themselves as such. The first was called James and came forward with outstretched arms. He had only one foot and yet he stood perfectly straight. There was just nothing at the bottom of his left leg. The next was quite old and cute. He had big, thick brows and a twinkle in his eyes. He was like a very old sage—wise, but mellowed.

Osgood was a straight haired man and quite thin. He might remind one of someone living in England who is a professor of science perhaps.

The next one looked like a lion. He said that he would be answering questions on our emotional states.

The last looked like Samson, very burly and strong.

Out of the group of five came a gentleman who was truly more like a mass of light. I could almost see a body through the mass. This man was called Bartholomew. He tells us that he was in the vibrations of this appearance a long time ago and worked long and hard. I "knew" this man quite well. I felt as if this was a reunion.

Bartholomew nods and takes the position of the doorkeeper. Aha, the real meaning of "Gatekeeper!" (See section on Automatic Writing) Just like an old friend, he reminisces about the houses that we have lived in and places where we have met. He explains that he has been available all of these years in between but it was not time to work together until then. He is grateful for the opportunity to again assist.

He demonstrates with his arms to his side, showing the palms of his hands. He shows us how energy may come from the palms and how much healing is there.

A book appeared in his hand. The colors were white, green and blue. The letters of the title and other markings on the book are in gold. He tells us, "*It is important that it be ready in manuscript form by June 1st.*" That is all he wants to say about this right now.

As I reviewed this material years later, I thought, I hope he hadn't meant 1986! The challenges and joys of daily living have taken me twenty years from that moment.

In closing he says, *"Do not think that you are ever alone. Only know that there are special people working for you and yours. I am happy to have made contact again. We will be present at all meetings (indicating the five). If you wish, we may do this once each month."*

Throughout this book, passages will be quoted from the trance work. The sessions spanned several months. I was always exhilarated, even if astonished, and very honored that the information was flowing through me. Bartholomew and the five messengers remained with me throughout my learning stages and in the early counseling sessions with my clients.

5

Symbolic Guidance

Our modern lives are chocked full of symbols. We cannot go through a day without them. So, it isn't surprising that much of the communication through the psychic senses is done with symbols.

When we drive a car, a simple stop sign evokes an automatic foot-on-the-brake response. On our computers, icons are used to do a variety of things. Arrows put us in the right direction.

In extra sensory perception we learn that symbols play a large part. Rather than words or sounds, or a moving picture, the message comes to us in a symbolic manner.

As a psychic counselor, I work with symbols that reveal far more of the situation than if the words or events themselves were shown to me. Here is an excerpt of a transcript of an actual session illustrating the symbolism involved. (This is used with permission of my client):

"As we enter into your level of vibrations this evening the symbol being shown is a really intricate and beautiful material, a tapestry. More than one person is doing the weaving. There are many threads and it is very possible that as we believe that we are the one in our conscious awareness pulling the one thread through our tapestry, our spectrum of lives is also being affected. With each step, each stitch that we put into that tapestry, many other pieces and many other levels are being completed and added to simultaneously. Yet we are only consciously aware of the one in front of us.

"The purpose is that all of life, all of our lives, through the now eternity, might be placed in the end of a pin. The vastness is minute, and the minute is vast. The difference is none. Perception and belief is all. There are no hidden doors; no hidden messages. There is importance and non-impor-

tance to the believer. We are guided by the totality of the tapestry, not by that which is in front of our physical eyes. We are motivated and are intent in the so-called now. Reality is processed a long time ago and brought forth through the now body. The intent and motivation has been there, if we can put chronological time on it, linear time on it, one to two-thousand years. It is very humorous because, how important is anything? And how unimportant is it all at any given moment."

Spirit, or the one who directs the session in the trance state, is speaking through me in symbolic terms. Often, if I attempt to explain or interpret I am merely putting my "spin" on it, when what is said may have a more profound significance to my client.

Here is another example of symbols in a reading: (Used with permission of client.)

"This person today that is called David, with his multiple lives as child, mother, leader, destroyer, captain, joker, has only to present himself for the satisfaction of the whole tapestry. There is no right or wrong stitch; there are just stitches that make up the tapestry. Were we to look at this tapestry one hundred years from now, then what is here would become part of what is almost like a three dimensional picture of the past with that time frame being visible with the naked eye. When one can begin to comprehend the magnificence of the entire tapestry, with acceptance of each moment, then one can begin to understand the conflicts that one creates for oneself in any given lifetime.

"As we view this tapestry with all of its physical lives woven into the whole, there are beautiful colors expressing each life. We read that the determined part of this one proceeds with caution. A sensitive ego in some areas, but not all, and it is as though the person here today vacillates on issues that keep him on the fence because the courage to bring full truth to the moment would strike the ego. It is as though there is a tiny knot in the thread that we are attempting to pull through that checks its progress. We must take a moment and examine the knot, and with love and tenderness loosen the thread, loosen its hold gently so it doesn't break, thus freeing it to move to the next stitch.

"Within the accumulation of souls, if you will, it would be for us difficult to look at the layer upon layer of the many lifetimes where karma was created and resolved. We will deal this day with those lifetimes that can bring benefit to the person now called David and the expression of the collected soul in his lifetime."

In this example, Spirit depicts a tapestry as a symbol and analogy of the many facets of a single life. Often I am not aware of what I say, but my client, the one whose vibrations my spiritual helpers are in tune with, knows what is intended to convey. As he takes the information into his own consciousness and events of his life unfold, the symbols guide and often caution the client in his decision to act or not to act.

Look around at the symbols you have co-created. Yes, even the things that you don't particularly like. Stand still for a moment. From the Source, the movement of energy becomes many vibrations and we direct the co-creation and it becomes the manifestation of our thought. It may show up as a chair, a plant, a person. It vibrates at different levels to hold it together in the most simplistic form.

Even the things we think are complicated are very simple. They were once ideas in the mind. You may ask, where do these ideas come from? Possibly they originate from this energy we call life.

Look around then at the symbols you have created for yourself. Do you really like what you see? Are you enjoying life? Can you honestly say to yourself that most of your life is joy? The symbols that we see are our creations, who we believe that we are, why we believe we are here and what we choose to experience in this lifetime.

Symbols are one of the greatest teachers that we have as we walk the planet Earth in these bodies. Symbols talk to us and teach us about the misconceptions we have about ourselves and our place in life. They direct us to examine where we came from and what significance that has for us. They teach us to look deeper, unfold more, to perhaps look at our integrity and our intent about life and where we are going. Symbols come to us in dreams from a place deep within us which purpose is to guide us to be all that we are. Symbols are the guideposts for change, for movement, for reflection. We are urged to take nothing for granted that is in our world.

A dichotomy comes into play here. That it is vastly important and that it is not important at all. In a sense, symbols are all that is, because it is how we perceive what we think we are, how we see the world and how we move in this energy at this time. Is it not all symbols after all?

The only world that there is, is what we perceive it to be. In a sense each individual views the world uniquely. What may be a symbol of love for one just might be a symbol for violence to another.

Another excerpt from the same reading for David:

"We are being shown a mailbox that looks tattered. It has been pounded, painted and designs have been affixed to it. It is really messed up. It is like you keep going to the mailbox and it is always empty, even though it changes color and shape. You cannot get the answer in a thing or a box. It doesn't come to you that way. What you are looking for is not there.

"Now, we are watching a ticker tape come out of your ear and we would ask you not to read it. Just throw it away. Don't read the ticker tape, but just let it come out and discard it. More than the mailbox and more than the ticker tape, we would ask you to go to your inner heart, the inner beating of your energy and listen. Be still and listen to know your truth and then ask for the courage to live that truth.

"You can demand and insist, but it will take giving that up. Let the heart of you, that essence that is you, guide you. How nice it is to know that you could surrender to that and just let go. It doesn't mean you sit. It will do what it needs to do with your permission. Listen and invite it to take over. It will signify that you are ready to hear your truth. You don't want to deny it. You don't want to instill upon it a scarecrow's view of the world.

"We are being shown a baby tiger. Because you are a tiger in your own strength, don't be afraid to be a baby one and trust that which is within you to take you through this lifetime. A child can do it. There is no scarecrow to justify, no pretense. It takes more courage than what most so-called adult beings have to relinquish the control they think they possess."

The dictionary defines the word, "symbol" from late Greek,: "*symbolon. A token or sign. Something that stands for or suggests something else by reason of relationship, association, or accidental resemblance. esp. A visible sign of something invisible.*"

In France in the 1880's writers and artists reacted against realism. They concerned themselves with basic truths, rather than something seen or said to be actualities. They were called Symbolists, who exalted the metaphysical and the mysterious and aimed to unify the art and function of the senses.

Ernest Holmes, founder of the Church of Religious Science and Science of Mind teachings, said this about symbolism: "*A mental impression denoting spiritual or mental truth. Most Hebrew scholars regard the Bible as an allegory, recording the spiritual advancement of the Jewish people. Jesus certainly thought it worthwhile to present some of his most important teachings in the form of parables. To him everything in the natural world was a symbol of some spiritual truth ... a representation of how the Cosmic Plan was working out in the unfoldment of man.*"

Your world does not look like my world—or anyone else's. We perceive things because of where we have been and what has happened to us in the present body, this lifetime, and physical expressions in other lifetimes. Sometimes that record in our head sets up a perception that may or may not be accurate.

There is that wonderful story of five people who witness an accident and each has a totally different account of the "facts" when they are asked to relate them. Who is to say which is the correct one.

We come from a variety of places and programming. We experience alone the moments of our lifetime. The symbols that we create daily are our very own. To think we can match up our symbols with someone else is to want false security on some level. As the other person identifies with our symbols we don't feel alone. It works as a validation for us.

James Redfield wrote in *The Celestine Prophecy* that the best course of action to follow was always one that *looked* brighter. Although the work was admittedly fiction it was based on Redfield's own experiences. To him and to many of his followers, the brighter, more colorful path became a symbol of the optimum way to proceed.

Our teachers in life are presented to us in symbolic forms: people, experiences and sometimes what we see as solid objects. They reflect back to us what we believe, what we recognize as our perception of what life must be. Then, too, we are symbols to others.

Something in our demeanor, our words and the manner in which we act and react that strikes an attraction from which another may learn the truth of who they are. We then are, in turn, teachers to others.

When something comes up in my life, I look for the meaning, or symbolism. It is occasionally that the significance is obscure and I will go into meditation to sort it out. Either I get an impression of what is intended, or the meaning will come to me by some unexpected action or event and make it all very clear.

A great deal of the trance work I did with my friend, Martha, was presented to me in symbols. During Trance Session #4 the following made reference to a specific symbolic lesson:

My voice on the tape: "I see a vast amount of people … they have no hair. I see all of these people but none have hair. Just a mass of them now are coming through the door. They are crowded together; there is not enough room to all come in at once. But they are in too much of a hurry. They haven't as yet learned what it takes to get through the door.

"It is like they are saying, 'Me first. Me first.' They would get through a lot faster if they would help the weaker ones go before them.

"A man comes out of the crowd and stands on the side. He tells me to observe what I am seeing. As I watch these people I realize they don't really love one another. They are going about it the wrong way. In their haste to be first they have bottlenecked and nobody is going anywhere.

"Now we are going around this crowd of people. It is though we are drawing a circle around them. Putting them in a big circle like a fixed block. They don't want to come out of their circle; they don't want to be able to move freely, or express freely. They find comfort in being shoved and pushed. This is a security to them."

And then I hear, "*That's a lesson.*"

We are all followers to a certain extent. The symbology of the lesson was not clear when it came out of my mouth, but in later years I gathered the knowledge needed to interpret it.

The first part is that everyone appears to be going somewhere and they all want to be there before anyone else. Sometimes we feel that we are in a race, but the destination is not outlined. The lack of hair was that we all look alike when there is no hair covering our heads. Our hair—its color, shape, texture, length, curl or no-curl—seems to identify us in an unique way.

The second part stirs a deeper feeling of our being. Helping the weaker people in our lives and putting them first is a by-product of unconditional love.

In my counseling practice I see a lot of the kind of people in the crowd in the circle. What they know is a sort of prison where they cannot express themselves freely, either physically or verbally. Doesn't this sound like the *victims* in this world? They are shoved and pushed and really don't want to break out of this victimhood. It is familiar to them. It is a security of a kind.

There was another trance session where the minute I got into it I was surrounded by all the symbols that I had been shown since I began the project.

There was the time that I saw a spotlight, like in a theatrical production. I felt as if I had turned into light itself. The feeling that I received was quite profound. The symbol was that I was becoming en-lightened!

The helpers, or guides, during my trance work would show me things in symbols many of which were not explained to me at the time but after pondering the symbol, Martha and I would be able to come up with a theory about what was shown to me.

The light depicted the expansion of light within me as an assistance for me to teach that we are bearers of the light and a beginning had been made by outlining for me what that feeling was like.

I remember a symbolic picture of a fish with its mouth open wide. Coming out of this fish was like a rolling movie film, continuously flowing from its mouth. Martha interpreted this to mean that there is a new age forming, which happens about every 6,000 years. We are coming out of the Piscean Age into the Aquarian Age.

Another time I was shown a wishbone laying upside down. The wishbone is the symbol of the Yogi—the tie between the physical and spiritual man. The Yoke.

6

Past Life Reincarnation and Karma

Have we lived before, in another life, another time, another body? That question had been on my mind for many years before I attended a past life regression class. I had heard about reincarnation and the arguments supporting the belief, but since I hadn't ever *remembered* living as someone in the past I had discounted it for myself. It never hurts to try out something new, especially since it could expand my ever-increasing knowledge of the supernatural.

I was skeptical and dubious when the director was introduced and he began explaining how past life regression was conducted. Curiosity encouraged me to raise my hand when volunteers were requested. For most of us, experiencing something new calls up an eagerness to learn more about life and living, and for all things that were considered "supernatural" I was always ardent and ready to hear about it.

The person who directed the regression sessions was a hypnotherapist who had taken many people back in "time" and forward into the future. Not realizing that I would be picked before I could witness someone else's session, I almost declined and asked the director to start with someone else. I was among friends who coaxed me into trying it anyway.

After being hypnotized and feeling relaxed and open I was directed to visualize a calendar. Since pictures were always in my mind that was an easy task. In my internal viewing screen, up popped a wall variety with squares for days.

He said, "Now, see the pages of the calendar flip backward into the past."

This was readily accomplished. Then, the director asked me to slow down the pages and stop, and describe what I saw.

As the screen cleared I found myself in a small house that was decorated in simple but expensive furnishings. I observed a young woman of about twenty years attending an infant. In the same room was the woman's mother who was grieving over the loss of her husband, my father.

I wasn't just remembering a scene, or watching another person's life like a movie, I realized that I was, or had been, that young woman.

Norway, with its blanket of stark white and sub zero temperatures, had taken my father's earth life. Before sadness engulfed me, the hypnotist instructed me to travel five years in the future.

I returned to that same house. Through a series of questions from the director, we learned that my mother had made her transition and that my husband, the father of my child, was one of the first Frenchmen to be involved in an import/export business and had an office at the docks nearby.

A woman appeared at my door carrying several books. She was there to give me my daily lesson in French. In an attempt to educate me, both socially and academically, my husband had hired her to tutor me.

I felt resentful about memorizing things I was never going to use. And it showed in my response to her teaching. Because of her frustration at my stubbornness and refusal to learn she would threaten to never return and flee from the house on many occasions.

My husband would try to persuade me, but I wouldn't listen. Convinced that I could not be educated, he told me that he was discouraged and weary and that he decided to send me to his parents in New Orleans. Since divorce was not permitted and the husband dictated what was what in those days I could do nothing but obey him. He coerced my brother into accompanying me so that it would not appear that I had run away.

Our journey to America was filled with cold, damp days of loneliness and despair. The men on board lived below decks while the women who could afford some luxury were billeted in upper cabins. In the hold were hundreds of people, families who were going to the promised land.

The plague hit the ship and took half the travelers. I am shocked to discover that among the victims was my brother, whom I had loved and nurtured since his birth.

The director moved me forward ten more years. I saw my home in New Orleans. My body lies limp on a bed and I am surrounded by my parents-in-law, a doctor and a housekeeper. As my spirit begins to leave my body I am aware of only the tremendous light that I move toward with a peace that cannot be equaled. The director quickly ended the session and I found myself awakening to a room full of curious faces.

When I returned to full consciousness I was awed and confused at what had just taken place. Was it a dream? Did I really live that life? Was it just a story that was in my unconscious mind? This was my first regression and I was not ready to accept the whole concept. For the next few days I experienced feelings and visions of that life that would come and go. Before long, however, the memory of it faded until it was out of my conscious mind.

Eighteen years later a friend and I were touring the United States by car and trailer. We had driven through the Midwestern states, up to Pennsylvania, down the eastern coastline to Florida, then over the state of Georgia.

When my friend suggested we stop in New Orleans, I was most uncomfortable. I had a knot in my stomach and wasn't able to figure out why I had a twinge of fear that came over me at the mention of that city. His persistence won out over my reluctance and with my solar plexus in an uproar, we continued on to Louisiana. By this time I had been in metaphysics for a number of years and knew that to ignore these sudden fears was only pushing a lesson, or a revelation, that would come up at a later date. Might as well face it and deal with it.

We arrived in the early evening and found a trailer park right away near the French Quarter. We wandered down the charming streets. Evening in the Quarter brought out many personalities milling around that could best be described as off-color. This did not appeal to me, so we headed back to our rolling home.

As we approached the trailer we had hauled for several weeks I hear myself saying that we could return in the morning because, "I really would like to see the inside of an apartment in the French Quarter." Suddenly, I was very curious about what was behind those beautiful, tall French doors and their wrought iron security bars.

"Oh yeah, right!" Said my friend. "One of the tenants is just going to ask you if you'd like to see his or her apartment. Sure."

"Why not?" I asked.

He replied with a question, "Are you aware of the large number of tourists that come here?"

Early morning on Bourbon Street is delightfully alive with vendors replacing products consumed by yesterday's shoppers and street cleaners whistling familiar tunes of the South.

As we strolled down the street, I said, "I think I like the Quarter in the morning."

We passed a lady in her middle years watering her upstairs patio garden. It was resplendent with flowers.

"Good morning," I said. She looked down and across the street to return the same greeting.

"The flowers look healthy and bright from this viewpoint," I called back.

"Thank you." She came closer to the wrought iron railing, leaned over and after a long eye-to-eye contact, she asked, "Would you like to see a French Quarter apartment?"

After muttering something about meeting me out in front of a tobacco store in a few minutes, my friend couldn't get away fast enough and was already a block away. He told me later that he was frightened hearing his words of the night before being repeated by a stranger.

As I crossed the street the nice lady, Alicia I would learn, was coming out of a door on the ground floor with an expectant look on her face. We introduced ourselves and she invited me to follow her. I had a feeling I already knew this woman.

Upstairs the floor space was much smaller than I had expected. I had an eerie sensation, but Alicia was so charming that I continued to follow her through her apartment. The living area was comfortable and attractive with a collection of artworks, massive pillows, a manuscript on a table that looked partially finished. And lots of those beautiful flowers I had seen on her patio, now cut and artistically arranged in vases and bowls.

At the bedroom door her voice trailed off as my body seemed to be going through an atomic disassembling, then reassembling process. Did a minute, or five, pass? I didn't know, but I stored the experience and picked up Alicia's voice again.

She was talking about her last book, *Psychic Poetry from the French Quarter*, and recalled how happy she had been when she was a professor at California State University at Fullerton—a town very close to my home. She then asked me when I was going to start writing books about my own psychic experiences. I hadn't mentioned that I had any paranormal abilities, nor did I say anything about my intentions to write about them. We talked for quite a while before I left to meet my friend.

During the time I had my first past life regression, and at this time when I visited that New Orleans apartment, there was no conscious awareness that the two experiences tied together in any way. It wasn't until several months later when I was driving through a remote area near my home in California that I received the full conscious impact of that time and space in the French Quarter. I pulled off the road and let my thoughts dwell on this, putting together the pieces that I now had.

My regression came full circle as I reviewed my passing in the bedroom of that house, now many small apartments. Alicia continues to play the role of housekeeper there after living a full and happy life. My mother of that past life had returned to assist me as my present Mother who was then finishing her responsibility to my handicapped son, who in that life was her son.

I thought about my intense motivation once I started to continue my higher education, the feeling of importance and urgency to be schooled in both social and academic matters. I said out loud, "So, that's why!" and returned to this world.

It was significant for me to observe that former dependent personality and the unhappiness she had caused. The knowledge gained helped me to prepare myself for interdependence in this lifetime.

What a wonderful tool we have with past life regression to bring us to an understanding of why we are who we are today. Life is a continuing learning experience if we pay attention to all of our experiences.

How does this relate to the ongoing expression of the soul? Very possibly the origin of the soul, in and of each of us, is birthless and deathless. It may have always been and will always be. Some feel that the soul's origination is at birth into a physical body. If that is true, there would be a dead end. Nothing in energy ever "dies!" God, as energy, is continually expressing Itself.

In the plant kingdom the soul is like a bulb that is buried in the ground to sprout up when the soil is ready. A new flower is born. Symbolically, the soul becomes a new physical body. When that body has had its time, it withers and dies, but the "bulb" remains to bloom again and again and again. Each expression can be compared, but no two are exactly the same. I don't believe that the bulb just lays in the soil awaiting to be expressed anymore than that the soul sits and waits to be expressed. Nothing is ever stagnant. The flower is never the same as the one that bloomed the year before and will not be the same as the one displayed the next year.

How could we think that there is a separation of the soul? I think ego does that. Ego wants us to believe that we remain "Aunt Mary," or "Uncle George" forever. The ego does not want to accept that it will be submerged and become part of the ocean of life, this oneness, that continues to express itself in so many forms.

Because energy vibrates at so many different levels there is no way we can "come back" as the expression we are in right now. I believe that there is a part of our soul that retains memory which allows us to access a previous experience in a past expression.

Why so many lifetimes? That is a question that has come up many times in my short life. I now believe that myriad lifetimes form a path to realization of who you really are.

7

Healing of the Soul and Body

To heal oneself or to guide others in the process is a natural ability that uses the Energy, or God's power, to change the thinking or attitude about the physical body, thereby allowing a return to its true state, that of wholeness or completeness.

The word heal means "*to make whole,*" from the Old English "*hal, whole or holiness.*"

Wholeness is a normal condition and can be sought, and regained. The body is always at work keeping the instrument going and fixing problems as they arise.

In my early practice I had seen such a difference in my clients who were getting well, or who were not. It seemed that there was an element between those who were into their illnesses and bought every symptom that accompanied them and the ones who appeared to be above their ailment who recognized and accepted it, but were looking for a way to be relieved of it. I found that the former stayed in their diseases despite the efforts of their doctors and other practitioners to bring them out of them. I found the difference to be in *belief.*

One rather dramatic example of healing occurred without my analyzing how to help or trying to figure out the workings of Spirit. I received a call from a client who was asking for help—prayer specifically—for her brand new niece. Only a few days old, her lungs had filled with fluid and according to the doctors, "death was imminent."

The new auntie had faith in me to know what to do and reached out for help. After the call, I immediately went into a higher state. That is, I closed my eyes, breathed deeply and went into deep meditation. I spoke the child's name and opened myself up to the Energy. On my inner screen I saw an automatic washer filled with water. By spiritual direction the tub began to spin, thereby spinning the water out. During the next two days this process was repeated. Each time, the water level in the imaginary tub was diminished markedly. On the third day my client called to report that the baby had made a turn toward recovery.

How do we explain these miracles? I certainly could not say that I did anything, other than have a deep trust and a belief. Jesus talked about the value of believing and having a conviction in the belief. That it would be done according to our belief.

From the book, *Healers on Healing*, a collection of writings by eminent metaphysical authors, comes a quotation from Ram Dass: "The conditions for healing involve faith in the possibility that healing can occur, and resonance with the deeper and wiser parts of the self where healing *is*." It is already inherent within us.

During a trance session, psychic medical information was shown to us, demonstrating that healing was a part of the blueprint for humanity. It began with this session:

(My voice.) "They are showing me all sorts of medical things. I see lungs that are dark. I don't know what this means, but I am looking at words being vibrations. These vibrations are cleaning up the lungs.

"This is for the future of mankind, he says. There are no defects."

*(*I think this is the voice of Bartholomew, speaking through me.*)"Take a physical body. Each little particle, or cell that the body is made of, lets in or rejects waves of darkness. Each cell has the capability of warding off this black cloud. If the cell, or particle, is not radiating light the black cloud sets in. This can be pulled away, or backed off. The radiating rejuvenates each cell to keep the cloud away. Thought material creates negativity."*

*(*My voice again.*)"* Jealousy. Resentment. Destruction. Anger. Hatred. I am watching these words come out of a person's mind."

(Another person's voice again.) *"But this black cloud forms from many minds, not just one, and as it floats through the air it attaches itself to a physical body. If that body is not prepared, a little piece of it enters and does its work. It is like this floating black cloud comes from the mind and goes back into the mind to be nourished and then it is strengthened to go out again."*

The director asked, *"How is the body prepared to resist this?"*

"Begin within the temple, the seed of the temple. It lies either dormant or full of light. When a black cloud approaches the body, if the seed is illumined, the blackness cannot enter. The seed is layered with each incarnation. There is the beginning, then a covering, and then another covering, and so on. All of these can be light or dark. The enrichment of the light seeps through the darker layers. When you have enlightenment, you have a rich, golden glow of brightness that the darkness cannot penetrate."

"May we be taught how to heal?"

(My voice.) "A man is going to a trough of water where he washes his hands. He shows me that they are clean. There is a strong light of vibrations coming off of his hands. There are two lights. He opens his hands so that I may see the radiance that emanates from his hands. The hands are then placed on a dark place on a physical body. The Light dispels this darkness and the body is healed. It would not be necessary for the hands to touch the body. The vibration is already strong enough and its power extends quite far from the hands."

Martha: "What does this healing? And does everyone have the potential for healing?"

"The power of God does the healing. All have the potential, but, you know there are qualifications here. He is saying that we can use the power. It is there. We must let it come through. When we prepare ourselves for it to come through us we will feel the power and we will know that it is successful."

"Can we do this now?"

"It has always been present. There is no hurry. How we waste time by trying to gain more. It will not unfold any faster than its own time. There

have been others and rumors of others who have done this. The power for healing can be done with vibratory rates without the use of hands."

It has been my experience that the palms of the hands emanate healing energy in and out of the body. I have used this method and have seen others do it.

I have also witnessed that a soul in stagnation, after crossing over, can be assisted to move on. This is a great healing tool. If we receive psychically the message that the entity is finished with this life and is ready to move into the next life experience, by all means it is our place to help that person gently go towards the light. We are always "in service" to each other at all times for soul learning.

There was a reference in trance session to healing by a man who in trance suggested treatment and care.

"There was a man in your country who healed the spiritual body and thus it was manifest in the physical." (I felt that he was referring to Edgar Cayce, a psychic who was active in the '20s and '30s and established the Association for Research and Enlightenment in Virginia Beach, Florida.)

"It is possible now. The power is there for all to heal when the instrument is pure. We have been given the direction this morning. Soon the Light will envelop the black clouds of doubt and fear."

Many healers in our history have used the power. Some doctors and other practitioners of healing use it unconsciously. We have heard of people getting well after the medical profession has given up. Belief and acceptance of a change taking place in the various bodies of energy cause the "darkness" to dissipate and allow the curative vibrations to restore wellness.

There were three main guides that helped me with my counseling over the early years. The one that assisted me with medical situations, as apparently in my over hundred incarnations I had never dealt in that field, was named Yul Ling. When he left to change his energy frequencies after twenty years I really missed his help. Then one day Ian and

Ilan came into my awareness. And they were with me for many years afterward.

I always advised my client to see a medical doctor, even if advice came through during our session that helped alleviate pain or suffering.

I counseled my clients in person, or on the telephone. Not only does it help to have feedback, the acceptance and understanding of what is given is crucial to the client making a change in order to heal a physical or mental problem.

Cooperation of the patient is essential in order to accept wholeness. If a second gain is not realized by the one who is asking for help and the person is sick of being sick and is ready to give it up, then a healing will manifest.

There is no "fixing" of anybody, least of all someone's husband, mother, friend or anyone other than the client.

PART III

THE FUNCTIONING ENTITY

1

Purpose of the Soul and Personality

Is there a purpose to the soul? There is much discussion about the soul. How do we know we have one? Can it be measured? Is it just a myth to frighten us as children into behaving and then to continue as adults? Some religions don't even acknowledge it. Others are all about the soul, saving it, losing it, or even having one.

During our first trance session (See Part II, Chapter 4), Martha and I asked the guides if there was a purpose to the soul. The one who answered first was called James. He spoke in metaphors and parables. This is what he said.

"The purpose of the soul might be compared to the mustard seed that is talked about by many and written in books. The seed always IS. It is planted and it grows, but it never dies. It takes diverse forms. It is constantly in movement and expression in one form or another.

"We might consider the soul in seed form when it is without a physical body. In its physical form we may see it as a tree or a plant that has blossomed and grown. However, the seed is the major source for the outreach, or expression. Sometimes a blade of grass, sometimes a flower, but when the seed is out of the shell we think of it as dormant. It is never dormant, but in another form.

"The reason for the soul to take on a human form is merely to express. It cannot stay out of body (in earth words) forever as it must always unfold. It continually expresses. And it is everlastingly alive—ready to burst forth in a new form. With great enthusiasm, with joy, it emerges into the new.

"Analogy can help you to grasp the soul's role. As a seed, it gathers unto itself other seeds of similar expression. We usually find roses with roses, pines with pines, and palms with palms. The form it chooses to take, the expression it imparts, and the like forms grouped together, assist us in understanding groups of individuals collecting together in order to experience the one Self."

I view it like the wheel of life that the sages talk about. The wheel remains the same—the soul. The soul's expression is the personality. Personalities are the spokes of that wheel.

When we begin to examine the functioning of the developing personality of an individual and its relationship to the expression of the soul, we have to start with the soul. It is never-ending, never-beginning, and as such remains the thing that survives the personality.

With recognition that the soul is the reason for, and the benefactor of, building up energy into a physical being and using it as a vehicle to carry that soul through a period of time on earth, we must question where the problems arise that are perceived by each of us daily in this life experience.

In most individuals there arises a conflict between the personality and the soul, a discord in what the soul has chosen to express and what the personality thinks *it needs to do, possess, or experience.* How much does the soul have to do with the direction we take? What does the developed personality, the "I", or who we think we are, have to do with what is actually accomplished in the progression of soul's growth?

What is the personality? I believe it is each lifetime a soul takes through which to express and grow. Our personality actually begins in the womb.

When the personality blossoms into expression it is pure and unprogrammed. Think of the personality like a computer disc, freshly formatted and ready to receive input. The soul has contributed traits and abilities, intelligence and a need to seek itself, just as a disc has attributes and inherent programs built into it.

Through visual, auditory and kinesthetic input, the imprinting of the personality continues. This can be from parents or others who raise us. Imprinting remains in operation throughout our physical lifetime. Input also includes information from geographical locations, race and other factors.

In the early forming stages, upon venturing out to other homes and lifestyles, the patterning of right/wrong, good/bad, increases with other examples to the inner program. The soul digests and rests.

In awareness, we begin to examine the programming that is forming to discover what is and what is not healthy for us. Not that the programming is incorrect but if it isn't working for us we need to take a look as enlightened beings.

There is never a separation of the soul, but there is a difference between the personality and the soul. If we were to look at the psychology of the situation and evaluate the personality, we would see energy blocks that prevent us from total unfoldment, from being all that we can be.

If we are still in that early programming stage where all our experiences are being written on the disc we are back to projecting, back to living in yesterday, back to the personality and to the ego. The soul awaits our realization of it. It waits for us to surrender to the guidance and construction of the soul.

Is the soul not Love? No matter what the personality does or is, there is nothing but Love from the soul. No judgement! No punishment! No reminder that there are should's, could's or have to's. The soul rests.

The trance session quoted above continued. The question was asked, "Where does the soul go when it is out of the body prior to incarnating again?"

The answer came without pause, *"It doesn't go anywhere!"*

The one who answered was a cute, rounded cherubic man with thick eyebrows and twinkle in his eyes. He seemed to be amused by the question.

"As humans, you perceive distance and time. Can you not accept that there really is neither? The concepts were accepted because of the human brain and the need to function in time, distance and space. All is now. Expressed in a variety of forms, but it is all NOW."

So, nothing happens outside of a time frame. In other words, the answer to the question of where the soul goes while it is awaiting another expression, if there is no time or space, then it cannot go anywhere. The wheel keeps going.

The late Jane Roberts, trance medium and well known author of the Seth books, wrote about there being several personalities "alive" at one time of an "oversoul."

See her fiction books, *The Education of Oversoul Seven* and *The Further Education of Oversoul Seven.* These books chronicle the lives of seven entities who "exist" at the same time. Their experiences and feelings mesh together at times and the learning that one of the personalities attains is felt by the others in varying ways.

The next question for my guides was, "What about the soul's desire to return to the light?"

The guide (I called this one The Professor) showed us first a pyramid with an eye at the top and mentions that the eye is usually lit. He says that he wonders if there is full understanding about the brightness of the eye at the top. He says,

"When the eye is open—not the physical eye, you understand—but when the eye is open the light is forever present. When through the tunnel of ignorance we stride and we see the light at the end of the tunnel, it is our belief and perception that takes us through the dark, black tunnel, except that the belief and perception of life prevails upon you. You are already IN the light. You are always in the light. It is the closed eye, the disbelief, the lack of faith, the distorted perception of this earth life that chooses the dark tunnel before the light."

We seek that which is all around us, within us, expressing through us! It is our acknowledgment of it and the conscious use of it that is the "Secret of Life," looked for all over the planet and into the galaxies.

My conscious mind must have been sleeping at the time, as it wasn't until years later when I read the actual words uttered that day that I came closer to an understanding of the soul and its purpose.

The answer to the following question, spoken by the director, brought me closer to the reality. "How do our emotional states block, or free, our full expression?"

This was from the one I referred to as The Lion:

"The emotional segment of earth life exists as a remainder of the surrendering process that is necessary for the expression and enhancement of the soul. Each time in the individual's emotional body a rejection or defense is present, energy is stopped, or dammed up, by that need and lack of acceptance of what IS. The clarity of the emotional body exists when through the eye of the beholder there is love and acceptance. When love and acceptance are not present, the emotional body rejects truth of what IS. Energy does not move through the stagnation that is created by rejecting and denying the reality of the moment.

"Whether animal or human, surely as the female is mother, so does acceptance of the now give peace and harmony to the expressed individual as with those that surround him or her. Emotions then are a warning signal of denial and to the degree that one accepts what IS—only to that degree—peace of mind exist."

It behooves us to work on accepting wherever we find ourselves. With love and openness in the situation, we then can begin to connect with the soul and discover its purpose in the present life expression. Then, harmony will prevail in any situation.

Many times I have fought with a situation only to realize at some point if I just stop and accept what is, ask what I can do to alleviate or change it, act on what my source tells me to do and then let go of it, the situation miraculously alters for the betterment of all concerned.

Sometimes my inner voice tells me to do nothing—and that works, too!

Having to do with the soul, the last question that was asked that day was, "How much does the developed, or developing, personality have to do with the soul's expression at any given time?"

The one who answered looked like a Samson.

"An analogy. In a house there are many windows and many rooms. Do not think that in any one lifetime all the rooms will be lit with light shining from all the windows. This is to dream in magnificence without reality. Know that a few lights are turned on each lifetime. When one can show his light without being in a human body, then all the lights are on in the house. There are but a handful that have reached that state.

"As grains of sand fill the beaches, so souls emerge, unfold and go back to seed. With each light the universe is lit. As each soul expresses love, joy, understanding, compassion, empathy, a light is illuminated. And the universe is beautiful.

Climb the ladder slowly. There is no time."

He holds up a clock with no movement, no hands.

"There is no time. When the personality is void like that of the clock, the soul can then be in command. The personality listens in humbleness. Each moment, each reality now, does the personality listen for the guidance of that which is within.

"Imagine, if you will, that there is one Seed. It is as though all that is expressed comes out of the one Seed, because there is no division. None. Between you and me, she and he, truly there is only One. Ask for guidance each moment along the way. Ask not of yourself, but of that which is within you."

The soul is always with us as an observer. Played out in a thought, an image, or a sound, it is up to us to pay attention. What can the personality do to acknowledge it?

The following is a brief quotation concerning the *Care of the Soul*, by Thomas Moore:

"We care for the soul simply by honoring its expressions, by giving it time and opportunity to reveal itself, and by living in a way that fosters the depth, integrity, and quality in which it flourishes. Soul is its own purpose and end."

Conflict is never without, but always within, between the developed personality/ego and the soul.

2

Know Yourself: Reality/My Truth

When we come into the awareness of a physical existence and can hear, feel and see, we enter with natural instincts and a clean slate of pure thought. We know absolutely who we are and have the desire to observe the experience.

There is an old story about a little boy whose parents have brought home a girl baby that he is supposed to call "sister." Several days go by as he observes the tiny, wrinkled thing. One day, he says to his mother, "I want to be alone with the baby for a few minutes." She thought, "Uh-oh. What does he want to do?"

It was finally arranged for the boy to have alone time with the new baby, with the parents in hearing distance and close by just in case. After staring at the baby girl for a long time he said, "Tell me about God! I'm starting to forget!"

Our tentative personality acts like a sponge, soaking up every little drop. After a time when we try to assimilate all of the new things we need to know about this life, we begin to forget how we came into being. We begin to put out of our conscious mind that which had gone before we incarnated into this present existence.

Imagine a clean, shiny disc that is blank. The personality begins to take on the effects of everything that is encountered, causing an imprinting process to occur. This process continues throughout our lives until the physical existence is terminated—unless we become aware of what is being imprinted and take action to consciously monitor and catalog each potential impress.

Our individual world is not like everyone else's. We perceive the world through our own filters accumulated throughout our lives, from where we've been and what has happened to us, and traditions and attitudes from our families and close relationships in this body and this lifetime. Sometimes that personal recording in our heads sets up a perception that may or may not be accurate. It would be different from anyone else's viewing.

Take a single incident that was witnesses by several people. Each one of those persons would have a slightly separate story to tell about it. Who is to say which story was the accurate one?

As an experiment, close one eye and look at an object with the other eye. Without moving your head, reverse the closed and opened eyes. Do you see the exact picture with both eyes? Look again! Alternate your eyes a couple of times. Isn't it somewhat changed—from a different point of view?

Just imagine what differences can result when two people with two eyes, and two ears, and individual imprinting, experience the same parents, upbringing and culture. Even twins have diverse reactions to the same stimulus. Different sex siblings not only are not raised the same, but they see things in their own characteristic perceptions.

Is it any wonder that any two people can have a happy, healthy relationship with all that has gone on in their respective lives?

Just trying to understand yourself is a lifetime endeavor.

When an "automatic" response begins to emerge and before you act on it, it is possible to alter the resultant response by asking yourself, "Is this an unconscious imprinting? Or do I really believe it (whatever is coming up for you)? Is it my Truth?

What *is* your Truth? We are bombarded especially in our formative years as to what is true and what is false in our purview. It is when we take in a word, or a whole circumstance, examine our feelings about it, make it a part of our experience, unique from other happenings in our inner universe, that it becomes our individual imprinting.

In everyone's expression there is an opportunity to just *be*, right here and now. If we are not just being—not doing, not acting or reacting—we are back to projecting, back to taping over and over, back to living in yesterday or tomorrow, or back to the personality. And so we miss out. Because we are in physical bodies with physical eyes and ears, we believe that this is all we are.

Aren't we apt to misuse our energy, if we don't live in the now? It is always there for us to use, the magnificence within us. If we filter everything we take in with that inner wisdom *before* we act on it, how can our response be anything but Truth.

I capitalize Truth because there is always only One Truth, no matter what the subject may be.

We cannot say that the personality is forever, just as we do not believe that our bodies are forever. But the soul is forever.

Get to know your own soul's growth; look at your own truth. Do you have any illusions that have been constructed of thin air, things that the ego builds upon a misunderstanding or an appearance, rather than a reality?

How about priorities that you have set up that are based on flimsy loyalties or false duties? Are they truly yours to complete? How do they affect your daily life? Are they interfering with your real purpose, that of your spiritual reality?

Go back to meditating regularly and focusing upon the True purpose of your being. You will not judge by appearances in your life, but use your creative thinking and permit your higher consciousness to be your guide.

Let the naturalness of your being, your psychic connection to the One, work through you for the betterment of not only your life, but the lives of everyone around you.

3

Co-Creator

By yourself you can do nothing. It is in your nature to think that you are alone in your endeavors.

How can you be by yourself when you never are? You are a part of everyone and everything. There is no separation. We are spiritual beings that hang out in these bodies that appear to be separate. In reality they aren't even by themselves.

With the energy that is available to us, we are co-creating everything in our lives. Energy that is everywhere present, in and through everybody, shapes itself into everything we see and experience. All of this is created with our thoughts, words and activities.

At the moment when we choose to go out of the physical existence, the Energy that leaves the body is incorporated back into the soul. Then that soul goes into another "house," as another entity. In a sense we are immortal. We live forever: we do and we don't.

Rosemarie will never be again. As long as she is in this body, she will be Rosemarie. She houses a soul and she is very grateful—sometimes through tears—to carry this body through its lifetime.

I will not be forever, and I will, because I will be a part of the incorporation of this soul within me, along with all of the hundreds of people I have probably been. So, where does ego really come in?

We have to let go of the ego—that is so very temporary and is kept alive by our stubbornness and naive beliefs—so that we can allow everything to come through us into manifestation. In this way we can change what we do not like about our lives. Magic? It is merely co-creating! *Which we are doing all the time anyway.*

Look around you. You have created everything you see and everything you are experiencing. It's not something or someone "out there" that has placed you where you are.

As you realize who you really are and release the little ego-self, things will begin to change. The most important part of that is: happiness and joy are all up to you.

It took me many years to know that I have created my life. And I am creating it still. When I was a child living in the coal mining town in Pennsylvania I knew I wasn't going to live my life there. People just survived; they didn't really live, because the only thing they thought about was a roof over their heads and food on the table.

I felt then that I was going to live in California. I didn't know anyone in California. And most people in that little coal town didn't even know where California was. My parents and friends laughed at me because they thought I didn't know what I was talking about. They had the belief, you know, that no one could change his or her life. That it was all directed by some large Creator who pronounced and exacted fate upon Its beings.

When I began traveling outside the continent of the United States I have to admit that I was never excited to go to other countries because in my mind there was nowhere I hadn't visited—if not this life, then other lifetimes. Part of that was precognitive, however, I had the belief and the visualization to see it, to co-create the experience. Our desire, coupled with the energy that is already available to us, and the knowing that accompanies it, has to manifest into fruition. So, when the belief is there and we can see it, feel it, and act upon it as if it already was, it simply is. We have to let go of the ego enough to allow everything to come through us. A lot of us block the good that is natural for us to experience.

We have to be careful when we use this energy because what we desire and pray for comes into existence. This is true with fear. "What I fear comes upon me!"

It will manifest itself. It has to. It is the law of cause and effect.

How can we criticize others unless we walk in their shoes? We don't have anyone else's soul inside of us. We don't know what is going on inside another person. It is difficult to allow others to follow their own path and to get into their own realization of who they are. Maybe they are not ready to accept who they are and believe that whatever happens, happens *to* them. In psychology this is called victimization.

In essence, we *do* bring it on ourselves because we co-create everything that shows up in our lives.

4

Harmony with the Universe

Being in harmony with the Universe is flowing with the Energy, the psychic energy of all Life. Problems develop when we start to go against the flow.

With joy, I realize we must also experience anguish. What we are trying to reach for is the natural way of everything, the flow of Life. I can only share with you my experiences and what has brought me to this day. It has been mostly in joy that I find myself right now. I have worked hard at it. I struggled through therapy while I was intuitively developing my psychic abilities that had hit me like a bomb. I didn't understand it and I was fearful of it.

I still have a lot of anguish. I get sad. The analyst in me comes forward. I recognize the feelings.

1) Is this something I can do something about?

2) Is this sadness of a situation that is happening now or memories of the past?

3) Accept what is and move on.

Denying a feeling denies our humanness in this Oneness of Life. Confront it head on before you go on. Then, I say to myself, "You've got about fifteen minutes to wallow in your depression! Then, get to work!"

There are times that depression can be a motivator; and sometimes it can be a barricade. The energy just seems to *whoosh* out and it would be so easy to just let the depression take over. We think we are protecting ourselves when we are depressed by withdrawing from the very thing we can be doing to ease the pain of it.

When we deny a part of us—the ugliness, that blackness in us—we are attempting to separate ourselves from the one energy that flows through all life. It vibrates at different levels, but it is still energy.

What we hear, see or touch is in beta consciousness, defined by scientific testing with an electroencephalogram. Other levels of consciousness we generally block out and call them "visions," "daydreams," etc. I have been in the psychic field more than forty years and what comes through me still amazes me. It sets me to wonder because I don't understand the mechanics of how it happens. I can't prove it.

I can't give you scientific proof that when I close my eyes and start breathing and shut down my left hemisphere of logic and reasoning, there is a whole other consciousness. In this awareness I hear, see and feel a difference and an inexplicable knowing comes to me. I believe that it emanates from the right hemisphere of the brain but I can't tell you how.

I get very curious about it. It drives me crazy. All I know is that it works. And, it works for everybody. When I do a reading I believe that it is the soul's energy that is being *read*, the depth and accuracy is uncanny.

There are ways that we place a barrier in front of this universal energy. Denial is definitely one of them. Denial of all that we are.

Regardless of where you have been, regardless of what you have thought or felt, you are a human being. As such, you are an expression of this energy in a human form at this time. So what does that mean? That you are constantly learning and growing and doing and being.

When you start to deny where you have been, what you have thought or what you have done, you have in a sense a dichotomy. You separate yourself in your mind from this flow of energy, although in truth there is never a separation.

This flow of energy would give you more joy, more love, more beingness if you did not deny and thus block it. If we look at the joy of psychic flow, we would say that it is a surrendering of all that we are—and what we think we are.

My surrender came early in life. If it hadn't I would have probably destroyed myself. Something so powerful, so insistent, so incipient had a hold on me and the more I tried to deny it, to run from it, the more it attached itself to me. My surrendering was for survival.

We separate ourselves. We are in heaven or hell in our minds. I stayed in the hell I created for myself for 32 years. No matter where I was, no matter what I was doing, I perceived separateness. I never felt a oneness, a connection, a joining, a Love (the capital is for the One Love that is I choose to call God). I didn't know what that was like. Life was very good to me. It gave me a turning point, a very traumatic experience, that jarred me into the realization that my little "hell" was not the real world—or the real me.

When I had that experience, I thought that it was certainly the answer. It certainly wasn't all the answers. I continued to live about the same; I continued to make the same mistakes in my decisions. Instead of having a masochist rating of "10," I was probably a "five." But, it wasn't over. No, it is never over. We are never finished because the Universe is never through with us. It is a continuum, continuous growing, learning and doing. For me, it is existentially a knowledge of being here, right now.

Another way to block our energy is to believe that we are done. Nothing can ruin or improve this model!!! Ha! Think again!

We have to be in this body at this time. Would you really like to be up on a mountain top sitting in a yoga position like a monk? Why? Who are you helping? What are you gaining? Not even your own soul's growth.

You can hide; you can refuse to integrate with other people. All that does is to cut you off from the psychic flow that I'm talking about.

If you choose to entertain the same thoughts; if you continue to accept the same beliefs and continue to act on that same belief system, *you live the same*! Day after day after day. Nothing will change.

There might be some security in that, I guess. Actually, I don't really think so. No husband, no wife, no job is going to give you security. *You* are your security. You take it with you.

Some people pay a very high price for what they feel is security. Our word. A very high price. Women sell their souls to men who will financially take care of them. Men, because they are afraid to find another partner, stay with the same person, the same job, and surround themselves with the same core of like-minded people—for security.

Change is frightening to most of us.

That is crazy thinking. Life is in constant flux. That's what Life is all about. If you stay in the NOW and experience the NOW, there is so much joy. You can enjoy the flow of Life in every moment.

Have you ever been with the "Remember when" people? You know, "when I was a child, this and that?" If you play that game, you will keep your energy "back there!" Not here, where creation sits.

You have the opportunity to change your life in thirty seconds—right now. In this energy flow you need only to change your thought. Make a new image for yourself. You've got to shut the door on that past stuff. Seal it and lock it. Then forget it!

At night when I go to bed I run a sort of film of my day. I think, God, I was awful in that situation. I don't like how I behaved in that situation. So, what do I do? I make a new tape of that experience. Right there and then I go over the day and I correct that behavior. I don't have to carry around that guilt. That blocks my energy, too.

I forgive myself! I forgive everyone involved! And then move on!

I look at my soul with such honor and love. I am never going to be here again, not as Rosemarie. I have been given such pleasure and privilege to carry this soul around and if I shut up long enough and listen, the soul will tell me what it needs to express, what it needs to experience. I am directed exactly where I need to be and what I need to do.

If your inner voice says to you, "go to Tahiti and learn to dance," *Go to Tahiti*! Learn how to dance! You will probably clear every cobweb you are carrying around with you. I am not saying you should do this to deliberately hurt somebody, as if to say, "Well, this is what I've got to do and to heck with you!" No, I am not saying that. I am just asking you to listen to the intent. Be truthful with yourself; look at your integrity.

It is not what you were taught to believe; not what your friends believe. When you are looking for your friends to confirm who you are, it is because you don't know. If you need somebody to agree with you all the time it is because you are not sure what you believe.

If you have a good friend who loves you and isn't experiencing jealousy or competition with you, they are going to say to you, "I think you ought to look at this." They won't agree with you if you aren't sure yourself. We need people who we can rap back and forth with, to bounce things off them.

We are talking about a letting go, a surrendering, to what you really are. This is the soul. This is the teacher within.

I think the whole trip is about finding out who we are. We all came here to do something, each and every one of us. We are individually special, very unique with our talents. There is so much I cannot do as a physical being and I am fascinated by other people's talents. Things I cannot do. I can do what I can do. This is when I am the most comfortable; this is when I flow; this is when I plug in.

When I am doing what I am guided to do by the flow of the universe my whole being knows it and feels it. If I allow myself to be in any situation doing anything where I am blocked and feel downtrodden, I am cheating myself. Remember, I am not coming back. I believe that my soul will and express itself as Jane, or Sara, or Michael, but there will only be one Rosemarie. So I had better live it fully. When I live it fully, the psychic part of me just resonates. It has to do that because it has no blockage.

Your body, your mind, your emotions—they are always wide open and ready to receive. All that is keeping the reception at bay is what we think we are, the ego personality that we need to let go. As tiny babies when we entered this plane the programming began, the picture began to be painted onto the canvas of our minds of who we think we are. This is done by experiences, parental examples, outside influences and in this era, The Television Set and all the other media that we are confronted with daily!

As we begin to pull away the facade of ego to reveal the true self by self examination, we are in constant struggle to retain the false "I." It is when we yield to the truth of our being that we receive the direction and peace of mind that the soul is always offering to us. Whether or not we accept it is an individual choice.

The *only* conflict is between the soul and the ego. We are not talking about separation, because there is no separation. The ego self, developed from birth to whatever age you are now, allows you to see and call you by what you think you are. Our ego is not to be denied because we have to live in it while we are in a physical body. However, it does battle with the soul.

It is only by looking at the soul's purpose, accomplished by shutting off our programmed ego through meditation, contemplation and quiet reflection. Then, we become aware that we project our personalities, that appear to be real. When we get past that hurdle, we begin to live in harmony with the universe and we can say that we are in the flow of Life.

5

Be Who You Are

Haven't I always been who I am? Do any of us know who we really are? The first thought is to state your name, but that doesn't tell anyone who you are.

According to the Bible, in his brief but dynamic life on earth, Jesus taught us that we are part of God, part of the Universe, part of each other.

"Know ye not that ye are gods? "If it was said in his instructions of what life is all about then it is absolutely true.

I really believe that the universe was built upon One Energy and that each and every creation in it is pure Energy. And every aspect of the Energy was meant to use that Energy. This is what and who we really are.

The ancient mystics taught this Truth. The "new thought" philosophies are based on this Truth. As we awaken to our true identity, dramatic positive changes will appear in our lives. Just the knowledge and awareness that we are more than we can see, hear and touch will stir an awakening.

With deep thought and meditation you can almost feel within you an expansion. You start to realize that it has been there all the time, just waiting your recognition.

Our wayshower, Jesus, spoke to the multitudes, telling us that we all possess the potential to do what he was able to do: "He that believes in me, the works that I do shall he do also, and greater works than these shall he do." The Holy Bible, KJV, John 14.12.

In a different chapter, said in another way: "If ye have faith as a grain of mustard seed … nothing shall be impossible to you." Bible, KJV, Matthew 17.20.

It is also written that we must believe and have Love in order to receive spiritual messages: "And though I have the gift of prophecy and understand all mysteries, and all knowledge, and though I have faith, so that I could remove mountains and have not charity (Love), I am nothing." KJV, ICorinthians 13.2

When we have sharpened our awareness and are able to see (clairvoyance), hear (clairaudience), and feel (clairsentience), we have a personal responsibility to use these gifts for good—for God—at all times and in every circumstance. We need only to enter the silence and listen to what Spirit reveals to us. Then, only with Love, can we impart our truth.

The very first step in using your spiritual senses—clairvoyance, clairaudience, and clairsentience (eyes, ears, and feelings)—is getting to know who you really are. Going deeper into this realization, begin to be aware of everything around you. Notice how each item presents itself, individually vibrating to the same energy, becoming a part of it, expressing its uniqueness.

Go outdoors and really experience a flower or a tree. Because it knows exactly what and who it is. A flower, for instance, merely unfolds and blossoms forth into the light as that specific variety in all its beauty. It knows not how or why it does this. It is simply being what it is.

The energy expressing through it is the same energy that is at the center and in every particle of your being. You may realize: a daisy does not try to be a gardenia. It radiates "daisy-ness" in all its cells.

Just be who you are. You are exclusively *you*. There is not another one just like you. Connect with that Presence inherent within your beingness. Know that there is no separation between you and the universe, no separation between creator and creation. Let yourself bloom into your spiritual uniqueness in all your glory.

For *that* is who you really are.

Bibliography

Addington, Jack and Cornelia, *The Joy of Meditation,* Camarillo, California: DeVorss & Co., 1979.

Carlson, Richard & Shield, Benjamin, *Healers on Healing*, New York, NY: Tarcher/Putnam, 1989.

Dyer, Wayne, *There's a Spiritual Solution to Every Problem*, New York, NY: Harper Collins Publishers Inc., 2002.

Einstein, Albert, *The World As I See It, Translated by Alan Harris,* New York, NY: Citadel Press, Carol Publishing Group Edition, 1999.

Hawking, Stephen, *A Brief History of Time, Updated and Expanded Tenth Anniversary Edition*, New York, NY: Bantam Books, 1998.

Rothschild, Fritz A., *Between God and Man: An Interpretation of Judaism*, from the writings of Abraham J. Heschel, New York, NY: Simon & Schuster, Free Press Paperback Classics Edition, October 1997.

Holmes, Ernest, *The Science of Mind,* New York, NY: Dodd, Mead & Co., 1938.

Leshan, Lawrence, *How To Meditate,* New York, NY: Back Bay Books/ Little, Brown & Co., 1999.

Moore, Thomas, *Care of the Soul,* New York, NY: Harper Collins Publishers, 1992, Warner Books, Inc., 1994.

Redfield, James, *The Celestine Prophecy*, New York, NY: Warner Books, Inc., 1993.

Roberts, Jane, *The Education of Oversoul Seven*, New Jersey: Prentice-Hall, 1971.

Roberts, Jane, *The Further Education of Oversoul Seven,* New Jersey: Prentice-Hall, 1979.

The Holy Bible, Authorized or King James Version, Cleveland, New York: The World Syndicate Publishing Co.

Tolle, Eckhart, *The Power of Now*, California: New World Library, 1999.

978-0-595-46533-0
0-595-46533-1

www.ingramcontent.com/pod-product-compliance
Lightning Source LLC
Chambersburg PA
CBHW051443280526
45785CB00003B/1409
* 9 7 8 0 5 9 5 4 6 5 3 3 0 *